QUIET RIOT

Quiet Riot

Nadia Finer

Illustrated by Holly Farndell

First published in the UK and USA in 2024 by
Moon + Bird, an imprint of Watkins Media Limited
Unit 11, Shepperton House, 83–93 Shepperton Road
London N1 3DF

info@moonandbird.com

Publisher: Fiona Robertson
Commissioning Editor: Lucy Carroll
Project Editor: Brittany Willis
Copyeditor: Claire Phillip
Head of Design: Karen Smith
Head of Marketing & Publicity: Laura Whitaker-Jones
Illustrator: Holly Farndell
Production: Uzma Taj

A CIP record for this book is available from the British Library

ISBN: 978-1-78678-843-6 (Hardback)
ISBN: 978-1-78678-921-1 (eBook)

10 9 8 7 6 5 4 3 2 1

Printed in China

www.moonandbirdbooks.com

NADIA FINER

QUIET RIOT

True Tales of Shy Superheroes Who Changed the World

ILLUSTRATED BY HOLLY FARNDELL

MOON
+BIRD

CONTENTS

INTRODUCTION

Hi there! I'm Nadia, a quiet person who often feels shy. I have a small voice that people tell me sounds weird, which makes me feel embarrassed and self-conscious at times. I know how to manage my shyness these days, but when I was younger, I hid at the back of a room and lurked on the sidelines. I preferred to keep my thoughts and ideas to myself.

In the past, I would avoid all kinds of things because I was so worried about being laughed at. I hated calling people I didn't know on the phone, and talking to groups of people gave me a stomach ache! Just the thought of being on camera made me want to cry. If only I could be louder and braver.

I didn't tell anyone how I felt because I was too shy. Have you ever noticed that people rarely talk about shyness? It's mostly ignored in day-to-day life. But the thing is, not speaking about shyness can make us feel *more* alone, like we're the only ones experiencing life this way. And that's not the case at all—there are lots of shy people, and many of them have done incredible things.

When you're shy, timid, or reserved—or whatever you want to call it—it's tempting to hide in the background of your life. It's easier and way more comfortable *not* to put your hand up, ask questions, share your opinions and ideas, or take a risk. But when we stay quiet and keep ourselves small, we miss out on all kinds of amazing experiences.

And here's the thing! When we don't join in, speak up, enter the race, or step onto the stage, other people miss out on what we have to offer. Quiet people have so many gifts and talents. It makes me sad to think we are keeping all that good stuff locked away.

Our quieter voices are missing from lots of important conversations: in the classroom, at work, in politics, and in the media. While there are some amazing shy people in every industry—and this book is full of them—there are many places where we don't have enough representation, and that is a huge problem. Often we have the exact skills and understanding to solve serious issues.

When I realized this, I decided to change how I thought about myself. I wanted to embrace my quiet personality and stop wishing I was different. It's OK to feel shy and awkward sometimes—it's part of what makes me human. I decided to start the Shy and Mighty Project because I was concerned that if I didn't do something to help other shy people, maybe no one else would.

I've studied everything there is to know about shyness, and I've given talks about it in schools and for big companies. I've also written about shyness in magazines, newspapers, and books. I've even managed to talk about it on the radio and TV. I found a way to overcome my fears and find my voice because I feel so strongly about this topic.

While working with my shyness, I wondered why people who achieve incredible things all seem so loud and outgoing. Where are all the softly spoken superheroes, leaders, innovators, and champions? Shy people need role models to realize they don't need to change. I decided to write this book to show that quiet people can be brave, successful, and awe-inspiring. It's the book I wish I had when I was younger—and the book I still need to keep me pushing forward.

This book contains 40 magnificent stories about the shy yet mighty. Athletes, writers, explorers, artists, singers, and activists from all over the world are featured. Importantly, each person has had to overcome their fears to find their voice.

Get ready to read about the remarkable achievements of music queen Beyoncé, racing star Lewis Hamilton, sporting wonder Lionel Messi, fashion icon Yves Saint Laurent, and many more! Their stories show that shy and softly spoken people can be trailblazers, and so can you.

The stories have been organized into ten sections—each one has an important message to help you start your own quiet riot. Start at the beginning of the book and read to the end, or dip in and out depending on your mood. You can read a story when you wake up, before bed or during a quiet moment in the day. It's up to you.

My heartfelt hope is that these stories will give you the confidence to try something new, stand up for your beliefs, and follow your dreams. Never forget that your voice matters and that the world needs to hear what you have to say.

With love,

Nadia

P.S. You can find out more about me, my work, and my books at

 www.shyandmighty.com

THE SHY AND MIGHTY

Manifesto

ALWAYS REMEMBER:

Shyness might make you feel lonely, but you are not alone.

Shyness is not shameful. Let's talk more about shyness.

Shy people are not broken. You don't need fixing.

Shy people have superpowers!

Shyness is not a weakness. You are mighty inside.

The world needs to hear your voice.

DREAM MASSIVE

Sally Ride
(1951–2012)

At the age of 18, Sally Ride was on track to become a professional tennis player, but on 20 July 1969, she found a new dream: going to space.

That evening, Sally should have been in bed asleep. She had an important tennis tournament the next day in her hometown of Los Angeles, California, USA, but something BIG was happening. On her screen was the grainy black and white footage of astronaut Neil Armstrong stepping onto the rocky surface of the Moon. He was announcing, "That's one small step for a man, one giant leap for mankind." Sally was entranced. Something people thought was impossible had happened. A man was on the Moon!

The next day, Sally won her match, but all she could think about was the space mission. It was as though a little star had started to glow inside her. Whenever she thought about space and imagined becoming an astronaut, the star would shine brighter.

When Sally studied science and mathematics at school, she felt strong and powerful. When she looked through her telescope at the night sky, that little star inside would burn brighter. And when people told her that science was not for girls, she ignored them. Instead, the star would shimmer and spark.

However, when Sally was in the classroom and her teacher asked a question, she shrunk. She would hunch over her desk and wish for the teacher to choose someone else. Sally often knew the answers, but speaking in front of everyone felt impossible! In those moments, Sally remembered her dream of being an astronaut, and the thought of going into space gave her a reason to be brave.

After graduating from school, Sally went to Stanford University to study English and Physics. She was the only girl on her course. At the time, the idea of a woman becoming an astronaut seemed bizarre to most people. Whenever she doubted herself, the star inside Sally would sparkle and remind her that she was capable, strong, and brave. With a name like Sally Ride, it seemed she was destined to blaze a trail across the sky.

In 1977, Sally was nearing the end of her university degree. She picked up a local newspaper—*The Stanford Daily*—and spotted something incredible. NASA had placed an advertisement on the front page announcing they were looking for people to become astronauts, and women could apply. The opportunity she had been waiting for was staring her in the face.

Deciding that this was definitely not the moment to be afraid, Sally picked up her pen. Imagining she was about to launch herself into a new kind of life, the star inside Sally sparkled. Sally filled out the application and sent it off.

After weeks and weeks of waiting, she was invited to attend a series of interviews and tests. They placed her in a tiny space to check she was not claustrophobic and put her through a multitude of examinations.

Sally then waited for months until she received a letter. It informed her that she and five other women had been chosen to join a group of 35 trainee astronauts at the Johnson Space Center in Houston, Texas, USA. Her combination of calm, intelligence, and sportiness made her perfect astronaut material.

That's when the hard work really started! Sally had to learn to parachute jump, move in a weightless environment, and navigate. She also had to

"*Whenever she doubted herself, the star inside Sally would sparkle and remind her that she was capable, strong, and brave.*"

become a strong scuba diver and swim in a heavy space suit. All the trainee astronauts had to learn to use the rocket controls and other complex equipment. Sally's favorite bit was flying a jet upside down at 500mph. The astronauts had to plan for every scenario and learn what to do if something went wrong. They would practice and practice until they got everything right. Sally loved learning new things and working as part of a team. She was in her element.

Five years later, Sally was chosen as a mission specialist for a six-day mission aboard the rocket-powered Space Shuttle. The press made a huge commotion! They asked her all kinds of ridiculous questions about makeup, underwear, and whether she might cry. Thankfully, the star inside Sally was shining brightly. She was too focused on her dreams to bother with their nonsense.

At last, the big day arrived. Sally was scared and excited as she sat in the spacecraft waiting for launch. Her dreams were about to come true. The countdown began, and 3, 2, 1 ... Lift off! On 18 June 1983, Sally became the first American woman—and the third woman worldwide—to fly to space. She was also the youngest-ever American astronaut. When Sally came back down to earth, she was a national hero. People wrote about her and featured her in songs and movies.

Sally made a second trip into space the next year and later became a professor of physics at the University of California, San Diego, USA, and the director of the California Space Institute. She made it her mission to encourage girls to get into the wonderful world of science.

Lionel Messi

(born 1987)

In the center of Grandoli—a small suburb in Rosario, Argentina—there was a soccer pitch made from dust and earth. Kids of all ages gathered there to play and let off steam. Stray dogs roamed the streets, horses trotted by, and people sipped cold drinks in the sun. The young Lionel "Leo" Messi, now one of the most famous soccer players of all time, lived nearby.

Leo was a small, timid boy who stuck close to his family. He avoided all the mischief and distractions of his neighborhood and rarely spoke to anyone. To keep him busy, Leo's grandmother asked if he could join in when some of the older boys formed a soccer team. He was only four years old, so the other boys seemed like giants! At first, Leo sat on the floor by himself and played with pebbles, but eventually, he looked up and noticed how they ran with the ball.

When the ball accidentally rolled over to him, Leo took a deep breath, gathered his courage, stood up, and tapped it gently. The ball rolled forward. He tapped it again and smiled. And that was it! He dribbled the ball as if it was the most natural thing in the world. The next day, he returned to the pitch and joined in without hesitating. Shy little Leo got the ball, ran toward the goal, and scored. Goal! He was hooked.

Leo's grandmother bought him his first pair of soccer boots so he could join the team. He was so talented that everyone gasped as he zoomed in and out of the other players. The ball was seemingly glued to his feet. And as for the goals—there were so many! Leo became known for miles around as the tiny goal-scoring wonderkid.

As well as being a skilled player, Leo was also considerate. During one game, he collided with the opposition's goalkeeper. He could have easily scored, but he left the ball and went to check on the keeper to make sure he wasn't hurt. Leo was a determined player, but deep down he was still a kind young boy.

Even though Leo was excellent at soccer, there was one main complication: he was much smaller than the other kids, even those his own age. He went to a doctor to find out why he wasn't growing and was diagnosed with a growth hormone deficiency. Growth hormone is a chemical-like substance made by a gland in the brain. It controls height as well as bone and muscle growth. To help Leo grow, he would need a daily special injection to increase the growth hormone levels in his body. This treatment did help Leo a lot, but it was expensive. The Argentinian government paid for a while, but soon, Leo's family would have to find the money.

Luckily for Leo, news of his talent was spreading far and wide. FC Barcelona (in Spain), one of the best soccer teams in the world, invited Leo to play for them. They also promised to pay for his treatment.

When he was just 13 years old, Leo and his family headed to Spain so that he could play for the Barcelona youth team. They were so impressed with him that his first contract was signed on the back of a napkin. They couldn't wait to complete the entire process! The coach there told the players to be careful with Leo. He was worried the bigger kids might injure him. But they just chuckled, "How can we hurt him if we can't catch him? He's too fast!"

Leo did not talk to his teammates for the first month or so. Moving to a new country, house, and soccer club made him homesick and even shyer. Leo found it challenging to settle in and make friends. He was also insecure about his body, so he got changed in private. It was a difficult time for Leo.

However, after a while, Leo started to feel more comfortable. Once the season got going, he began to relax and chat with people. He made friends and had fun. Leo *loved* the game. He did like to win, but mostly, he wanted to play soccer for the joy of it!

Leo turned his quietness and his size into his superpower. Even today, when he gets the ball, his aim is to swerve as many people as possible. He dodges, tackles, and darts around the other players. He's good at going unnoticed until it's too late to stop him—then the ball is in the back of the net!

Leo doesn't care about being famous or having lots of fans or followers. He is more concerned with scoring goals. His unique approach to the game is what makes him one of the best soccer players in the world. Go, Leo!

"*Leo turned his quietness and his size into his superpower. Even today, when he gets the ball, his goal is to swerve as many people as possible.*"

Jessica Watson

(born 1993)

Jessica Watson is the youngest person to sail solo and unassisted around the world. She accomplished her dream at just 16 years old, but it wasn't without years of practice and preparation.

The first few times Jessica's parents took her sailing, she didn't want to go! Jessica was a timid and cautious kind of kid. She was worried about the icy cold water and did not like the idea of getting drenched. Too scared to join in, she sat and watched her brother and sisters as they glided across the water.

Feeling unsure was familiar to Jessica. She was afraid of climbing trees, going too fast on her bike, and jumping into water. Fear controlled Jessica's life and stopped her from trying new things, joining in, and having fun.

But there was no escaping sailing. Jessica's life was changed forever when her parents sold their house and business to live on a boat and sail the Australian Gold Coast. Instead of going to school, Jessica's mum taught them as they sailed. The family would go camping and spend lots of time outside. Gradually, Jessica realized that trying new things could be enjoyable. She saw that being on the water was safe, that sailing was fun, and gave her freedom!

Jessica has a learning difficulty called dyslexia, so her mum would read stories out loud to her. One of the stories was about a man who sailed around the world all by himself—a normal person who had achieved something incredible. As Jessica listened, her eyes opened wide.

The story had planted a seed in Jessica's mind, and she felt inspired to start nurturing her new dream. Sailing around the world seemed like such a big challenge. Could she do something scary like that? Jessica could not help but wonder.

Jessica didn't share her thoughts with anyone because she was worried about what they would say. After all, she was only 11 years old! She feared they would squash her dream. But when she finally felt brave enough to tell her parents, they didn't laugh or tell her off. They encouraged her to start planning.

For four years, Jessica devoted herself to sailing. She took lessons, studied books, and learned about safety, engines, radios, and first aid. She also learned about the weather and how to sail in different conditions. There are no repair shops at sea, so Jessica had to learn how to fix and rebuild equipment if it broke. She was still rather shy and reserved, but Jessica had to ask the more experienced sailors for advice when she needed it.

And then there was the small matter of buying a boat! Boats can cost vast amounts, and the one she needed was particularly expensive. It was as watertight as a submarine and had lots of safety features and gadgets—such as solar panels and a satellite phone—to make sailing it as smooth and safe as possible. Jessica worked various odd jobs to earn money, and mustered the courage to ask companies to sponsor her trip.

When the boat was ready, Jessica did a test run. On the first night, her boat crashed into a huge ship while she was sleeping, and the mast was snapped in two. Jessica was upset and embarrassed at the mistake—it was a terrible disaster.

Tempting as it was to run away and hide, Jessica managed to steer her thoughts to focus on her goal and the valuable lessons she had learned. There will always be setbacks. The important thing is how you recover from them.

Finally, on 18 October 2009, Jessica set sail on her journey around the world from Sydney, Australia. The plan was to take 210 days to cover almost 23,000 miles. She was just 16 years old!

Jessica was by herself aboard her boat, which was called *Ella's Pink Lady,* for the entire journey. She only had her books and music for company. The rules stated that Jessica wasn't allowed to stop and nobody could come onto the boat to help her. The only way she could talk to people was via her radio and the blog she wrote along the way.

The trip was not always plain sailing. Jessica forced herself to put on "happy glasses" during difficult moments so she could see the best in a situation and appreciate the good things.

She faced rough seas, massive waves, and battering winds. During the long and lonely voyage, Jessica had to carry out many repairs to the sails, stove, pump, kettle, and even the toilet! At times her little boat struggled, and it was knocked down over and over. One night, conditions were so rough that the boat smashed into the sea four times. Luckily, the damage was not too serious, and Jessica was unhurt.

Aside from the danger and the drama, Jessica's journey was filled with epic beauty and breathtaking moments. She saw the sun rise over the sea, watched whales leap, and gazed at the night sky filled with dazzling stars.

After eight months, Jessica returned to Sydney and was met by 75,000 people cheering her on. Jessica had become the youngest person to sail solo all the way around the world without stopping. Her incredible journey shows us that all adventures start with a dream and the courage to talk about it.

Anthony Horowitz

(born 1955)

In the 1950s, in London, England, there was a boy who lived in a house so big that when it was eventually demolished many years later, 16 gigantic houses were built in its place.

Growing up in a massive mansion with lots of money, fancy cars, and expensive things sounds amazing, right? Unfortunately, this wasn't really the case for Anthony Horowitz.

Even though his house was massive, it was miserable. Anthony's father could be cruel and distant. Nobody knew where all his money came from, and when he died, nobody knew where it all went. He left behind huge debts, and there was a lingering suspicion that he'd been up to no good.

When Anthony was young, his father often mistreated him. He was made to perform for his father's important guests by telling jokes and was forced to prove his intellect before he was given dinner. And Anthony's grandmother was so gruesome and awful that she made everyone who entered the house afraid of her.

During all this misery, Anthony's mother provided a glimmer of love and affection. When she was able to get away from her husband and mother-in-law, she read him horror and adventure stories. These fleeting moments were precious indeed. Otherwise, Anthony was ignored and isolated with only the nanny or the driver keeping an eye on him.

His only happy place was his father's library. Anthony felt safe in the library surrounded by books. He spent hours reading, writing, and fantasizing

about another life, a life that was overflowing with adventure and fun—and far away from his family. The pictures in his mind came to life as stories on the pages of his notebooks, giving him hope for a brighter future.

Unfortunately, Anthony's next real adventure bore no resemblance to his dreams. One day, without warning, he was shipped off to a boarding school and left to fend for himself. The school was run by old-fashioned and often cruel teachers who seemingly enjoyed making the boys' lives a complete misery. They even used corporal punishment, which means they hit misbehaving students with belts or sticks. Thankfully, this horrific practice is now illegal in lots of countries.

To say that Anthony hated the school would be the world's biggest understatement. He despised it more than congealed custard covered in bogies! In fact, when he went back to his school many years later, it brought back such terrible memories that he was nearly sick.

To cope with his horrible situation, Anthony would sit in class and let his imagination whisk him away to far-flung places and take him on exhilarating adventures. He thought up tales of double-crossing spies, murderous mysteries, and do-or-die detectives.

After being punished cruelly one day, Anthony offered to tell everyone in his dormitory a story. He wasn't used to being the storyteller, so he started his tale rather shy. As Anthony gradually found his voice, his confidence grew, and the words began to flow. He spoke of spies, monsters, and bad guys being defeated. There were giggles, guffaws, and gasps. Under the cover of darkness and duvets, Anthony had started to shine.

"There have been many times that Anthony has worried about being successful or speaking in front of crowds, but in those moments, he remembers that his voice matters."

At that moment, Anthony knew he wanted to become a writer. He felt it was his destiny, so he wrote and wrote and wrote! He shared his stories at night, designed intriguing book covers, and even practiced his signature so that he'd be ready to sign books for his fans. Writing stories gave him hope. They gave him a power and a future. It didn't matter whether his father or his teachers believed in him. Anthony was determined to make it happen and become a great success. And he did!

Anthony is now a bestselling author. He's written over 50 brilliant books, including the popular *Alex Rider* series. His books have even been made into plays, films, and TV programs. He writes stories of survival, determination, hope, and defeating ghastly grannies and terrifying teachers!

There have been many times that Anthony has worried about being successful or speaking in front of crowds, but in those moments, he remembers that his voice matters. His stories bring hope and excitement to young people everywhere, no matter what they are going through. After all, it's hard to feel lonely when you are reading a brilliant book!

DREAM MASSIVE

Quiet Reflection

Take a moment to reflect on the
previous chapter and answer these
questions to help you work out how
you can dream massively.

I have the most fun when I am . . .

The things that are most important to me are . . .

I want to feel . . .

I want to learn . . .

I want my life to be . . .

If I knew I could not fail, I would . . .

I feel like there's something glowing
inside me when . . .

My biggest dream is to . . .

When I think about my dream, it makes me feel . . .

The first step I am going to take
toward making my dream
happen is . . .

BE KIND TO YOURSELF

Zendaya
(born 1996)

When American actor and singer Zendaya was young, she loved going to work with her mother at the local theater. Watching the actors tell stories and create imaginary worlds on stage was like magic. She would sit alone in the dark at the back of the theater with her snacks and watch from afar. It was Zendaya's happy place.

When she was at school, Zendaya also liked to sit at the back of the classroom. She would observe everything and not put her hand up, join discussions, or ask the teacher for help if she got stuck. She would even hide in the bathroom at lunchtime to avoid having to speak to the other children. Zendaya hardly spoke at all.

Zendaya's parents and teachers were worried. They wanted to help her come out of her shell, but they did not know how. With the help of a counselor, her parents hatched a plan to help Zendaya find her confidence.

Their big idea was to encourage Zendaya to try lots of new things. There was no pressure to stick things out, to be good at anything, or even like the things she tried. The goal was simply to try new activities and see what happened.

Zendaya bought into the plan and joined lots of clubs. Sometimes she had fun, and sometimes she did not. Occasionally, she uncovered hidden talents such as basketball, dancing, and singing. Zendaya became an expert at taking small risks, and bit by bit, everything seemed less scary.

Zendaya continued to enjoy singing and dancing, but only from the safety of her bedroom, where nobody could see her. Hearing their daughter upstairs,

"The moment the spotlight landed on Zendaya, something inside her changed. It was as if she had turned from a silkworm into a glow worm."

her parents recognized how talented she was. They did not want her to stay hidden away, so they urged Zendaya to try stepping onto the stage for fun. They told her she had nothing to lose and that her performance did not have to be perfect. If she did not like it, she would never have to do it again. Zendaya agreed! Her first acting role was as a silent silkworm in Roald Dahl's *James and the Giant Peach*. She had no lines, which was perfect for her stage debut.

The moment the spotlight landed on Zendaya, something inside her changed. It was as if she had turned from a silkworm into a glow worm. She was the best and most expressive worm the audience had ever seen! Even though people were watching her, all her fears and inhibitions disappeared. On the stage, Zendaya could be anything she wanted.

Following her wonderful worm performance, Zendaya immersed herself in the theater. She joined a drama school and learned all about acting and scripts. She also discovered how to understand characters and use her body and voice. Her first proper acting role was as one of the witches in *Macbeth* by William Shakespeare. Zendaya discovered that being reflective helped her understand the characters she was playing. Being shy definitely enriched her performance.

Zendaya's big break came in 2010 when she was given a part in the TV program *Shake It Up* on the Disney Channel. She became a teen idol, singing hit records and launching fashion lines. Since then, Zendaya has also acted in an award-wining TV series and in movies such as *The Greatest Showman* and *Spider-Man*. She has won awards, recorded an album, and written a book, too!

Zendaya is still shy, but she has learned how to deal with her nerves and cope with large social gatherings. She practices talking to new people as if she is preparing for a part in a play. Zendaya accepts that she might feel awkward in a new situation—and that it might be a bit difficult—but she does it anyway because she knows the results will be worth it.

She also still loves to try new things, such as painting. Rather than putting pressure on herself to be great—or even to be any good at all—she enjoys being a beginner and learning new skills.

After a busy day on set, where she has to speak to lots of different people, Zendaya returns home and relaxes by watching her favorite TV programs or hanging out with her friends. Being around familiar people comforts her and makes her feel safe so she can be brave again the next day!

James Earl Jones

(1931–2024)

James Earl Jones was a renowned stage and screen actor. He grew up on a farm in Michigan, USA, with his grandparents and his large family.

One bitterly cold winter's day on the farm, snow blanketed the ground. There was lots of work to do, and everyone had to pitch in, even little James. Suddenly, his young uncle had a seizure. Poor James was terribly frightened. His grandmother told him to run to the nearest road and get help as the farm didn't have a telephone. Fearing for his uncle's life, James scampered through the snow as fast as he could.

He made it to the local store, and luckily, they had a telephone. James opened his mouth to ask the shopkeeper to call a doctor, but no sound came out. He could not speak. He needed to save his uncle, but the words wouldn't come. That was the day James started to stutter.

From then on, whenever James tried to speak, his voice would get stuck on a specific sound, and the words would get wedged. People laughed at him, so to avoid stuttering, James stopped talking for a long time.

James accepted that he was now someone who didn't speak. Instead of talking, he wrote whatever he needed to say. At school, his teachers would let him write down his answers. In some ways, he enjoyed the silence, and he quite liked reading, observing, and listening. James became a budding poet, and if he ever felt shy or awkward, he simply hid behind a book.

Eight extremely long years passed in silence, and then one day at school, something happened. James had written a poem that impressed his English

> *"Rather than feeling embarrassed or ashamed about the remains of his stutter, James learned to love his unique, rich, and powerful voice."*

teacher. He challenged James to prove it was his poem by reciting it out loud in front of his classmates.

Because it was his own work and they were his thoughts on the page, James managed to speak it without stuttering. It must have been strange for him to discover that his voice had transformed so dramatically. When he last spoke—such a long time ago—he was a little boy. Now, his voice was deep and booming!

James' teacher encouraged him to keep working on his speaking skills so that he could share more of his poems and writing. He even encouraged James to get involved with debating and drama, which is not something he could have imagined a few months earlier. When James was on stage pretending to be someone else, he could relax and let go of his fears and inhibitions. Little by little, his stutter started to fade away.

Over the years, James practiced speaking to make it easier. He found that reciting his own poems helped a lot, and in 1957, he stepped onto the Broadway stage for the first time. He only had three lines, and he did stumble a little, but he got through it!

James worked hard to figure out ways to manage his stutter. In time, he could deliver big speeches and recite all his lines both on stage and in front of the camera. James found that acting and having a script made it much easier for his words to flow. He avoided the sounds and words that made him get stuck, even changing the words in the script if he had to. Slowly, he overcame his obstacles.

James went on to star in hundreds of films and plays and win lots of awards. He became one of the most instantly recognizable voices in the world. He will always be remembered for being the voice of Mufasa in *The Lion King* and Darth Vader in *Star Wars*.

James still stuttered sometimes if he felt particularly emotional, but he kept going. Rather than feeling embarrassed or ashamed about the remains of his stutter, James learned to love his unique, rich, and powerful voice.

And what a voice! The fact that he went from being completely silent to becoming one of the most loved and recognized voices of all time is truly remarkable.

Yuna Kim
(born 1990)

Yuna Kim is a South Korean competitive figure skater who has won loads of awards and broke numerous world records.

Yuna was a very quiet, shy girl who did not like talking to people she did not know. Worries and fears wrapped around her, stifling and smushing Yuna's spirit. When she was a child, a new ice rink opened in the province of Gyeonggi-do in South Korea, and her family were keen to discover what the fuss was all about. It had been a while since they had had a fun day out.

Yuna borrowed some skates from her aunt. They were too big, but she did not mind. Spellbound, she gazed at the people gliding around elegantly on the ice. When she stepped out herself, Yuna felt a flurry of both anticipation and fear bubbling inside her. Trying new things was not easy. She was wobbly at first, but within a few moments, Yuna was floating across the rink.

A skating coach spotted Yuna and was impressed by how gracefully she moved across the ice. He wondered if Yuna could become a skating champion and suggested that she join some classes. At first, Yuna wasn't sure what to make of this stranger, but her family seemed to trust him.

Even though it was expensive, Yuna's parents agreed to let her learn to skate properly. They worked hard to pay for her lessons, and at first, she had to wear old skates held together with tape. Yuna didn't mind, though—she was in love with skating! She adored the feeling of freedom as she danced on the ice. Skating made her feel strong and powerful. By the time she was ten years old, she could jump in the air and spin numerous times before landing perfectly on the ice. Wow!

Having natural talent was fantastic, but for Yuna to become a champion, she would need to devote herself to ice skating. She battled blisters and the biggest, bluest of bruises from the inevitable falls as she practiced—but Yuna was committed. All she did was eat, train, and sleep. She never skipped training because she knew that the hard work was necessary.

To progress, Yuna had to enter competitions. However, because she was shy and self-conscious, she found competing stressful. She struggled to relax and let go of her inhibitions. When Yuna performed, she was all alone out there on the ice, isolated and in the spotlight. There was a lot of pressure on her to be perfect, and many people were staring at her, scrutinizing her every move. She struggled to jazz up her performances under this pressure. Poor Yuna felt so awkward!

Luckily for Yuna, her coach understood—he also knew what it was like to feel shy. Instead of focusing on what could go wrong, he encouraged her to think about how skating made her feel. When she connected with the music and the emotion in the melodies, Yuna could perform freely and find her own style.

As her confidence grew and her skills improved, Yuna won more and more competitions and championships. Yet, no matter how many opponents she beat, she could not fully overcome her nerves. During the warmups, her legs would shake, and she wouldn't be able to jump. She would be overcome with panic.

One day, Yuna realized that being a champion was much more than being a spectacular ice skater. She would need to become a champion on the inside, too. So, she set to work on building herself a mighty mindset.

Yuna had to learn to relax and realize that feeling nervous is normal. She thought about all the work she had put in and imagined herself doing each of the moves perfectly. She began to accept that it is OK to mess up and make mistakes sometimes. The world does not end if you're not perfect. Knowing this helped Yuna to relax and enjoy her skating much more.

When Yuna's self-belief dipped, she would look to world champion figure skater Michelle Kwan for inspiration. Yuna adored Michelle and admired her confidence on the ice. She wanted to be just like her, so she spent hours studying her training routines and performances. When she skated, she would pretend to be Michelle—just thinking about Michelle boosted her bravery.

There was a lot of pressure on Yuna's shoulders, particularly when she made it to the Olympics. Thousands of people were in the audience, and millions were watching on TV. Yuna tried not to think about all the fans and their expectations. She tried to relax and have fun.

Yuna Kim was the first female skater to win all the biggest competitions—the World Championships, the Four Continents Championships, the Grand Prix Final, and, of course, the gold medal in the 2010 Winter Olympics. She broke the world record 11 times, and one day, she got to perform to a song called "Hero" with Michelle Kwan. It was a perfect moment.

"Yuna realized that being a champion was about much more than being a spectacular ice skater. She would need to become a champion on the inside, too."

Wolfgang Puck
(born 1949)

Famous chef Wolfgang Puck grew up on an isolated farm in the Austrian hills with his sister, mother, grandmother, and stepfather. Their house was very basic—the toilet was outside, and there was no running water!

The family home wasn't a happy one. Wolfgang's stepfather was an alcoholic with a terrible anger problem. The family lived in fear of his explosive temper, and they were always worried about what he might do or say next.

Wolfgang felt like his stepfather's critical voice was inside his head. The louder the cruel voice became, the smaller Wolfgang felt. He became so shy and withdrawn that he wanted to disappear completely.

The only time that Wolfgang and his family felt safe was when they were in the kitchen. This was because his stepdad had no interest in cooking. They spent hours sheltering from the turmoil in the warmth of that room, cooking up a storm, and making meat cutlets called wiener-schnitzel and mountains of mashed potato.

In those days, there were no ready meals or pizzas. Everything was made from scratch. If Wolfgang wanted one of his mother's legendary hot chocolates, they would have to milk the cow, skim the milk, and make the chocolate. It would take half a day!

To keep out of his violent stepfather's way, sometimes Wolfgang would wake up before the sun came up. Around four o'clock in the morning, he'd sprint across the fields to a nearby farmhouse to seek refuge.

Wolfgang knew he needed to get out of the house and move away. He couldn't continue living in such a frightening place, so when he was just 14 years old, Wolfgang left home and vowed never to return.

He found work in a restaurant, peeling potatoes and washing dishes. Even though he had escaped his stepfather, the negative voice was still stuck in his head. It told him he was no good and would never amount to anything.

Wolfgang worked hard in the restaurant and did his best, but one day, he didn't peel enough potatoes, and the chef lost his temper. He shouted at poor Wolfgang, telling him he was useless and a total disaster in the kitchen. Wolfgang was fired on the spot and booted out onto the street.

Humiliated and terribly upset by the outburst, young Wolfgang did not know what to do. He could not face going home under any circumstance and felt like a total failure. This was a rock bottom moment. Wolfgang wondered how he could carry on. The world seemed like an unforgiving place, and he wanted to give up.

But Wolfgang made an important decision. He reminded himself that bullies do not have the right to control others. He deserved much more than the treatment he had received. A dogged determination roared and rose within him and silenced the negative voice in his head.

Wolfgang knew that he was good at cooking. He was going to become a chef and would not let anything or anyone get in his way. Nothing could stop him from pursuing his goal.

The next day, without telling anyone, Wolfgang snuck back into the restaurant's cellar and continued peeling vegetables! After a few weeks, the chef discovered Wolfgang chopping in the cellar. He was so angry that he screamed at Wolfgang to leave.

But Wolfgang did not back down. He was used to bullies and knew that if he went home, he would face someone even worse. So, he stood his ground and told the chef that he was not going anywhere. Once he had calmed down, the chef could not help but be impressed by Wolfgang's determination. He gave him his job back.

Over the years, Wolfgang climbed up the cooking ladder until he became a head chef. The horrible voice in his head still whispered to him, telling him that chefs were meant to be loud and shout a lot. It told him that he was not good enough. Sometimes, Wolfgang struggled to make eye contact with people or chat with his customers, and this made the negative voice get louder.

However, Wolfgang managed to stand up to the bully in his mind. He thought about what really mattered: his love for cooking and making people happy with food. Instead of squashing who he was, he focused on causing a stir with his talents.

Wolfgang opened his own restaurant called Spago in Hollywood, California, USA, and it soon became a hotspot for famous movie stars and glamorous celebrities. He became known for creating a posh kind of pizza with salmon and caviar!

When he was first invited to go on a TV cooking show, he was not sure if it was what he wanted. The idea of being on screen scared him, and he found it hard to look into the camera. But the more he did it, the easier it became. Over the years, millions of viewers all over the world have fallen in love with the kind, gentle chef.

BE KIND TO YOURSELF

Quiet Reflection

Pause for a moment and think about the stories you have just read. Now answer these questions and work out how you can be even more kind to yourself.

When I take care of myself, I feel . . .

My perfect day starts with . . .

I like to relax by . . .

When life feels noisy and loud, I find quiet by . . .

I feel happiest when . . .

I feel snuggly and safe when . . .

I feel loved when . . .

If I was my own best friend, I would tell myself . . .

In my life, I need more . . .

It's important to look after
myself because . . .

LET GO, LET iT OUT!

Albert Einstein
(1879–1955)

The world-famous physicist Albert Einstein did not like making mistakes. He was worried that his words would tumble out in a jumble, so he would repeat them in his head before he spoke.

When he was young, he didn't speak for the first three years of his life, and it was a few more years after that before he could speak fluently. Trying to understand how things worked was Albert's passion. He spent much of his time alone playing with puzzles and building steam engines. When he was four years old, he was given a compass to play with. He tipped it this way and that, noticing that the needle always pointed to the north. He wondered what was going on and resolved to figure it out.

Surprisingly, for such a deep-thinking young boy, Albert did not breeze through school. He was a shy, socially awkward child who struggled to talk to people, let alone make friends. Albert didn't like being told what to do and couldn't concentrate, often distracting the rest of the class. His brain functioned in a different way to the other kids. He skipped classes and messed about, and his teachers couldn't stand him! They said he was a rebel who would not amount to anything, and they kicked him out.

It was a harsh blow for someone who was already worried about not being good enough. But, once he had left school, Albert blossomed. He was finally free to focus on the scientific theories and ideas that interested him. He experimented, analyzed, and investigated, frantically scribbling his ideas on a blackboard. Alone in his laboratory, he could try new things, make mistakes, and correct them in a safe and judgment-free zone.

Over time, Albert's confidence started to grow. Still, whenever he met other scientists, he would feel intimidated and worry that he didn't know as much as them. In those moments, speaking felt almost impossible. When other people disagreed with his theories and ideas, he was far too shy to argue with them—or explain how he was, in fact, correct.

Einstein was a physics pioneer. He developed new ways of thinking that would change how we think about science and the world forever. When he did have the confidence to speak, people started to listen, and when he published his groundbreaking papers, people paid attention. Universities fought over him, and he was offered jobs at many important places. People traveled from all over the world to see him, and then in 1921, Albert won the biggest science prize of all: the Nobel Prize. This made him a science superstar!

When he was a young boy, people had teased Albert for being different. But now he could see that being different was a good thing. He decided to be himself and embrace his quirks. He let his hair grow wild and decided he would never wear socks again. He went full Einstein! For Albert, physics was much more fun than fame. People would often recognize and stop him in the street, but he would pretend he just happened to look like Einstein and walk away!

Albert turned down interviews and invitations because public speaking made him nervous and uncomfortable and even caused him to stumble over his words. He passed up party invitations by making excuses and hiding at home instead. He asked himself why he needed to speak to so many people. Why couldn't he just stay home reading his books and thinking about the wonders of the universe?

Eventually, it dawned on him that, although he didn't like fame or the attention that came with being a genius, if he hid away, his ideas would stay hidden, too. Worrying about making mistakes and not believing in yourself doesn't help anyone—and his ideas were big and important. They needed to be shared, not stuck inside his head or written on his blackboard. Albert had to conquer his fears.

Albert started to travel—just a little at first—and then gradually more. He enjoyed spending time with new people and sharing his ideas. On one trip to America, he met all kinds of celebrities and influential people. He even became friends with Charlie Chaplin, the famous actor and filmmaker. Albert realized that true friends don't try to change you. They support you and love you just the way you are.

Albert was staying at Charlie's house in America when he had an incredible idea. He snuck off to study and spent two weeks locked away on his own. Eventually, he emerged bedraggled and stinky, having written his famous theory of relativity, which explains how space relates to time. Imagine if he'd never found the courage to travel to America and meet his friend. He may never have explored all his ideas!

Emily Brontë
(1818–1848)

From the very start, author Emily Brontë's life was filled with sadness and loss. When she was just three years old, her mother died, leaving her devastated father to look after their six children.

Emily and her siblings—Maria, Elizabeth, Charlotte, Anne, and Branwell—had a hard life growing up on the Yorkshire Moors. They were battered by wind, rain, sickness, and the kind of cold, soggy dampness that seeped deep into their bones.

Despite the harsh weather, Emily loved the moors. The family house was surrounded by a bleak and brutal wilderness, but when she was outside, Emily felt rooted, like she belonged there.

When they weren't helping around the house, the children kept busy by writing stories and conjuring up magical lands. They drew maps, illustrated characters, and wrote long, incredibly detailed tales in tiny handwriting. They filled page after page with poems and stories.

This suited Emily. She was a shy, quiet girl who barely spoke. She preferred to listen and watch. Emily enjoyed being in her own head, rolling ideas around and building stories. Her mind bubbled with thoughts and ideas.

Mr Brontë was worried about his children, so he thought he was doing the right thing when he shipped them all off to boarding school to get an education. But the school was freezing, musty, and spooky, and there wasn't enough food. Unsurprisingly, they got sick. And then a tragedy struck—Maria and Elizabeth caught a disease called tuberculosis and died.

Emily was heartbroken. First, her mother had died, and now her sisters. Life was so unkind and unfair. She wished she could hide herself away at home, where she felt safe, surrounded by family and familiarity. Her sister Charlotte dreamed of escaping, but Emily wanted to stay home alone, living in her imagination and writing stories.

Along with her enormous slobbery dog named Keeper, Emily would trudge across the gray, gloomy moors for hours and hours, no matter how wild or wet the weather—her unruly, curly hair billowing in the wind. She explored scary places and discovered wild beasts, always searching for inspiration and weaving stories in her mind.

The years passed, and Emily became more and more reclusive. She hardly ever left the house except to go for walks with Keeper or to go to church —and that's how she liked it. When visitors came to the house, she found the conversation so awkward that she often hid behind doors or even under the table. If people spoke to her, she would not respond.

The idea of anyone else getting sick was unbearable to Emily, so she threw herself into caring for her family. She kept busy with laundry, cleaning, and cooking. She liked these daily chores because they were boring, and while she was baking or scrubbing, she could let her imagination run wild. There were always scraps of paper in her pocket or on the table,

"Emily enjoyed being in her own head, rolling ideas around and building stories. Her mind bubbled with thoughts and ideas."

and she'd stop every few minutes to scribble down her ideas. Gradually, these stories took shape, and Emily started writing a book set in Yorkshire, the land she loved.

One day, Charlotte was poking around when she came across a book of Emily's poems. Without asking permission, she read them. Emily was furious. Her poems were private! Eventually, Emily calmed down enough to listen to her sister, who told her how good they were. After much persuasion, Emily agreed to publish them, but only if the other sisters published their work, too, and only if they could use fake names.

So, Emily Brontë became Ellis Bell, Charlotte was known as Currer Bell, and Anne used the name Acton Bell. They only sold a couple of copies of their poetry collection, which was rather disappointing, but it was the first step!

In 1846, aged 27, Emily finally finished writing her novel, *Wuthering Heights*, and published it under the name Ellis Bell. Set on the hostile landscape of the moors, it is a wild and bleak love story about a man called Heathcliff and a woman called Cathy. It's considered one of the greatest books ever written, and now the author's name on the front cover is Emily Brontë. The mysterious girl who hardly spoke a word finally found her voice through writing and influenced millions of people all over the world.

Steven Spielberg

(born 1946)

When he was six years old, the now-famous movie director Steven Spielberg and his family went to the movie theater to watch a movie about a circus and the lives of the clowns, trapeze artists, and elephant trainers who worked there. In one scene, there was a dramatic train crash.

Afterward, Steven was brimming with questions about the movie, especially the crash. The pictures were stuck in his mind, and Steven could not forget them. He tried to recreate the collision with his toy trains by smashing them together repeatedly.

Disturbed by the noise and distressed by the damage, his mother dug out the family's video camera. She suggested that Steven film the collision so that he could watch it as much as he liked without destroying his toys —or her eardrums!

That day, Steven made his first-ever film. He also discovered that looking through the camera lens helped him make sense of his feelings and the world around him.

Steven grew up in a comfortable home with his parents and three sisters in Ohio, USA. He was treated very well at home, but outside the house, Steven was shy and awkward. He found it hard to make friends. The Spielberg family stood out because they were Jewish in an area where nobody else was. At school, kids mocked Steven and even beat him up. Sometimes, people would walk past the house and shout horrible, hateful things at the family. Steven felt like a stranger who did not belong.

"Even though he was shy, Steven's dreams of making movies were too strong to resist. They stomped all over his fears."

Yet everything was different when he held the video camera in his hand. Watching the action through the lens allowed him to be involved while staying safely on the sidelines. Steven started capturing every moment on film. After school, he spent hours writing scripts and editing scenes.

Unexpectedly, it turned out that creating movies was a good way of making friends. Steven was inundated with boys and girls desperate for a starring role! This gave him an idea. Steven cast one of his bullies in a movie and gave his part an untimely end covered in exploding flour. He left Steven alone after that.

To get inspiration, Steven went to the movie theater whenever he could. Over time, he became more and more creative, using all kinds of special effects. He particularly liked making scary films about monsters with gooey, blood-like ketchup spurting all over the place.

When Steven was 12 years old, he filmed a whole movie with actors and a script, and when he was 16 years old, he made a full-length science fiction movie about aliens. His family were so excited and proud. His dad even hired out the local movie theater for a night to show the film on the big screen.

When his family moved to California because of his father's work, Steven was lucky enough to visit Universal Studios. He could not believe that he could see professional people making actual movies!

From then on, he went to the studios whenever he had spare time. The security guards were impressed by his enthusiasm, so they let him hide backstage and peek through the curtains to watch the films being made. It was an incredible opportunity. He was right there, in the thick of the action.

Even though he was shy, Steven's dreams of making movies were too strong to resist. They stomped all over his fears. He threw caution to the wind and found the courage to talk to some of the people who worked at the studios.

Despite his nerves, Steven introduced himself to the filmmakers and explained that he made movies. They loved his dedication and offered him some work experience in the studios. He made a short film called *Amblin'* about two kids who go on an epic road trip from the desert to the seaside. It impressed some important people and won two prestigious film awards. As a result, the bosses at Universal Studios offered him a job with a seven-year contract.

Even though Steven is super famous, he doesn't enjoy attending big parties or shouting about his achievements. However, his success is hard to ignore —Steven is the most famous film director of our time, making many phenomenal movies and winning numerous awards, such as Oscars, BAFTAs, Emmys, and Golden Globes. His famous movies include *Jaws, Jurassic Park, Indiana Jones, Hook, Men in Black, The BFG, and Schindler's List.* He is especially famous for using jaw-dropping special effects that go way beyond spraying everyone with flour or ketchup!

One of Steven's most famous movies is *E.T. the Extra-Terrestrial,* a story about a boy who makes friends with a lovable little alien trying to find his way home. If you look carefully, you will notice that Steven's movies often explore feelings of loneliness and belonging, which he knows a lot about.

Lang Lang (born 1982)

When he was a toddler, little Lang Lang was sitting in front of the TV in his living room watching *Tom and Jerry*. The cartoon cat and mouse played the piano and chased each other up and down the keys. Lang Lang was captivated by the beautiful classical music, the piano, and the playfulness of the characters.

Lang Lang's family loved music. His dad played a traditional Chinese violin and organized an orchestra. His mum loved singing and dancing, and together, they would perform for family and friends every weekend. It was so much fun, and Lang Lang loved to join in.

When he was three years old, his dad bought him a piano. Music helped him feel like he was part of something and express himself. And as it turned out, he was extremely talented! By the time he was just five years old, he had performed in front of crowds of people he didn't know and won a local piano-playing competition.

Lang Lang's dad saw a lot of potential in his son and was determined that he should become a brilliant pianist. He put all his effort into supporting his son's musical talent, but he also put a lot of pressure on him—far too much pressure, in fact.

When Lang Lang was nine years old, he had to wake up at 5 o'clock in the morning and practice playing the piano before going to school. After he got home, he would practice again. In total, he would play for five hours each day! There was no time for making friends or playing games. Lang Lang felt like he was chained to the piano.

Lang Lang longed to make friends with children his own age, but all this pressure made him feel anxious and shy. He withdrew inside himself, isolated and alone.

That year, Lang Lang's father took him to Beijing, the capital of China, to see if he could get into the Central Conservatory of Music, a music academy. What could have been a fun road trip turned into a distressing experience for Lang Lang. The teacher his father had sought out declared Lang Lang had no talent and they should go back home. Instead of being compassionate, Lang Lang's father was furious. He behaved awfully, frightening his son with his reaction and telling him his life wasn't worth living. He had taken the rejection personally—it was as though his dreams had been broken, not his son's. Lang Lang wanted to give up playing the piano for good.

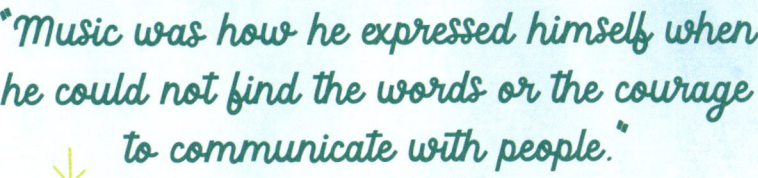

"Music was how he expressed himself when he could not find the words or the courage to communicate with people."

Lang Lang's father eventually calmed down and took him home. He found him a new teacher—this time, someone who believed in Lang Lang and encouraged him not to give up. Lang Lang realized that he was very good at playing the piano and that he wasn't trapped by it. Quite the opposite, in fact! While playing, Lang Lang felt like he was transported to a world where he could be anything he wanted to be. A world where his imagination could run free. Music was how he expressed himself when he could not find the words or the courage to communicate with people.

So, Lang Lang decided to take control of his dreams and make them his own. He worked incredibly hard every single day. But it was different this time—instead of focusing on his father and the things he wanted, Lang Lang centred on his own dreams. He played the piano for the love of the music, his future, and his freedom. The piano was his life, his voice.

A few months later, Lang Lang tried to get into the Central Conservatory of Music in Beijing again. This time he succeeded! His playing improved daily—he was learning from the best piano teachers in China and was free to develop his unique style. He found that on stage—in front of hundreds and even thousands of people—he overcame his shyness and felt powerful.

Lang Lang is a huge success! He sells out concerts all over the world and plays for famous, highly esteemed orchestras. He's played for presidents and even performed at the Beijing Olympic Games opening ceremony in 2008. Lang Lang's style is flamboyant and unique. Emotions run through his fingers onto the keys. Nobody can control him, nobody can silence him, and, importantly, nobody can tell him what to do!

LET IT GO, LET IT OUT

Quiet Reflection

Sit down for a moment and think about if, like the people in this chapter, you have something you need to let go or let out. Use these questions to help you reflect on your answer.

When I feel shy or self-conscious,
I am often worried about . . .

I have been missing out on . . .

If nobody was watching, I would . . .

If I could speak my mind, I would say . . .

My favorite way to express myself is . . .

From now on, I am going to make sure I . . .

I have a great idea. It involves . . .

The person I want to tell about it is . . .

I feel inspired when I am . . .

My voice matters because . . .

BE TRUE
TO YOU

Beyoncé
(born 1981)

In the 1980s, a little girl named Beyoncé lived in a nice house in Houston, Texas, USA. She lived with her sister Solange and their parents, Tina and Matthew. At first, Beyoncé loved going to school. She was a quiet, studious kid with a passion for solving perplexing puzzles.

However, there was one problem in Beyoncé's life that she couldn't solve. A group of girls had started to pick on her for being shy and quiet. They called her names, made fun of her ears, and intimidated her. Her school became a horrible place to be.

Beyoncé did everything she could to disappear into the background. Even if she knew the answer in class, she would stay silent. She kept her head down and tried to be invisible. People thought she was unfriendly and even arrogant. Nobody knew the truth—that she was being bullied. But while she was quiet and reserved on the outside, Beyoncé was silently building big, beautiful dreams in her mind.

Unsurprisingly, Beyoncé's mother was worried about her. She signed her up to a singing and dancing class in the hope that she would rebuild her confidence and make some new friends.

At first, Beyoncé was too shy to join in, but her teacher was smart—she promised Beyoncé a dollar if she would sing a little. And when she finally did, Beyoncé was dazzling. Her teacher was amazed!

Soon after, Beyoncé's teacher encouraged her to sign up for the school talent show. Beyoncé was terrified. She'd never stepped foot on a stage, let alone

performed in public! When the day came, Beyoncé went out despite trembling and feeling queasy. Then, after what felt like a very long time, the beats kicked in, and something magical happened. The timid little girl who barely dared to speak blossomed like a flower and transformed into a mighty pop powerhouse!

As she belted out the final note, the crowd went wild. They rose to their feet, clapping and cheering. Beyoncé's parents were in shock. They couldn't believe what they were seeing. Was this smiling, shining, confident performer their daughter?

After that, Beyoncé won 35 talent shows in a row. She was an unstoppable force! Fame and fortune were beckoning. When she was invited to join a group called Girls Tyme she leapt at the chance to sing professionally.

The girls in the group worked incredibly hard and practiced as much as possible. When an opportunity to sing for some judges on a TV show arose, Beyoncé was convinced that this was her shot at fame. They performed well, but the judges didn't like them. Their dreams had been dashed, and the poor girls were devastated. Beyoncé didn't want to give up though—she knew that things don't always go according to plan.

Sometimes people don't understand you, and that's OK. Sometimes people don't like you, and that's OK, too. The girls remembered that when life chucks lemons at you, you make lemonade!

They picked themselves up, renamed the group Destiny's Child, and got back to work with renewed determination. This time, Beyoncé wrote songs, designed outfits, and choreographed routines. She was all in!

And then, in 1997, the group signed a record deal with Columbia Records. They catapulted to fame, won awards and secured hit after hit with records like "Survivor", "Say My Name", and "Jumpin', Jumpin'".

Beyoncé loved being part of a group and performing with her best friends. It was like being on an all-singing, all-dancing summer vacation every single day! She spent almost all her time with her bandmates, and when they were together, Beyoncé felt invincible.

However, away from the stage, Beyoncé still felt shy and awkward. She found talking to lots of people extremely hard and hated dancing at parties. When she had to go out for dinner, she imagined slipping under the table and sneaking off!

Eventually, the girls went their own separate ways, and Beyoncé faced a new challenge: singing solo. After being with her friends for all those years, the thought of standing alone on stage and performing as a solo artist made her tremble. If only she had superpowers!

Beyoncé imagined a light coming down from the sky and entering her body to give her incredible powers. She imagined transforming into a fearless, fiery, flamboyant version of herself. She called this alter ego Sasha Fierce. Sasha Fierce could do anything. She could sing any note. She dazzled everyone and was everything Beyoncé wanted to be if she wasn't afraid.

Every time Beyoncé stepped onto the stage, she let herself feel as though she was Sasha Fierce by channeling the character's qualities.

As the years went by, Beyoncé became more comfortable on her own, and she realized she didn't need Sasha anymore. Beyoncé was ready. It was time for her to step up and shine as her true, magnificent self!

Paul Cézanne
(1839–1906)

In the mid-1800s, in a lovely little French town called Aix-en-Provence lived Paul Cézanne. You may have heard of him as a famous French artist, but back then, he was a quiet, sensitive young boy.

Paul was different from the other boys, which they unkindly reminded him about on a regular basis. One day at school, another boy named Emile Zola was being pushed around. There was no way he could defend himself, and Paul was not about to stand back and watch him get hurt.

Paul shoved the bullies out of the way, grabbed Emile by his jacket, and hauled him to safety. Naturally, the bullies were put out, so they went after Paul, but he shrugged it off.

Emile was so grateful for Paul's kindness that he gave him a big basket of juicy apples to say thank you. From that day forward, Paul and Emile became best friends. They were inseparable. While the other boys would spend hours in cafes, playing cards and dominoes, Paul and Emile would get up at dawn to go on long walks. They often disappeared for days.

Young Paul dreamed of becoming an artist, and Emile longed to be a writer. Paul would take a sketchbook on their hikes and often stop to draw something spectacular that he had spotted. They would laze in the shade to study the intense colors and light all around them and discuss their hopes and dreams for the future.

When he wasn't out walking, Paul spent every spare moment painting and drawing. He found infinite beauty and inspiration in the world around him

and was especially fascinated with apples. He would paint them hundreds and hundreds of times, noticing fresh details and nuances every time.

Eventually, Paul told his mother about his ambitions. She was encouraging, but they both knew there was a big problem: Paul's father. He had come from a poor family and had worked incredibly hard to build his hat-making business and set up the first bank in their town. He hoped Paul would become a lawyer and have a sensible career.

At first, Paul tried to please his father, even enrolling in law school, but try as he might, he could not ditch his artistic dreams. Feeling very sad, he moped about the house with a face like thunder. Although he had stood up to the bullies that day at school, he could not stand up to his father.

Eventually, Paul's mother came to the rescue by persuading her husband that Paul should be allowed to apply to art school. Twice, he applied, and twice, he didn't get in. Paul was devastated. He felt like a failure. His ego was bruised, and his dream of becoming an artist hung in the balance.

Then, he remembered the apples! He hadn't just painted one apple; he had painted hundreds! So, if art was his life, why would he give up now? He packed his things and headed to Paris, the capital city of France. He was eager to start his new life as an artist. Even though he worried about making friends and feared being alone, his dream gave him the strength he needed to take a risk.

Paul found a little studio where he could paint and then looked around for inspiration. He was dazzled by the paintings he discovered in the famous art museum, the Louvre, and humbled by the talented artists he met, such as Auguste Renoir and Claude Monet.

He desperately tried to get his paintings accepted to the prestigious art exhibition known as the Salon, but the judges did not like or understand his rugged painting style. Paul wondered if he should put down his paintbrushes once and for all.

Finally, after so much rejection, he decided to make a change. Instead of changing his style in an attempt to impress the critics, Paul chose to be himself. He headed back to the sun-drenched landscape of the South of France. After all, the vivid blue sky, glittering sea, and dazzling sunshine were his first inspiration!

He soon set to work and found that his passion had returned. Paul became fascinated with the mountain called Mont Sainte-Victoire, painting it over 80 times from all different angles and in different lights. He painted furiously, from dusk to dawn, producing thousands of paintings.

At long last, people in Aix began to purchase Paul's paintings, and then word of his talent began to spread further than the south of France. People in Paris and beyond were clamoring to procure a painting by the incredible Paul Cézanne! They admired and appreciated how he used color and shape and his unique, rebellious style.

Meanwhile, his old friend Emile Zola had become a famous writer. The two friends had been right. They were destined for great things, each in their own unique way. Today, Paul Cézanne is considered by many to be the father of modern art. In 2011, one of his paintings sold for an incredible $259 million—the most expensive impressionist painting ever sold!

Agatha Christie

(1890–1976)

Young Agatha was down in the dumps. She was stuck at home on her own yet again as her much older brother and sister were at school. She wasn't allowed to go—she had to stay home instead. Sure, she was lucky to live in such a big country house in Devon, a picturesque area of England, but Agatha was fed up with being left behind with just her pets and imaginary friends for company. Agatha was a quiet, shy girl, but that didn't mean she wanted to live a boring life. No way.

Agatha ached for adventure. To relieve her boredom, she spent her time reading books, inventing games, and writing stories. She let her ideas run wild and created characters of her own. Starved of human company and with no real friends, books provided Agatha with the mischief and mystery she longed for. She learned to read in secret when she was just four years old. Her mother hadn't wanted her to read till she was eight.

Agatha dreamed of a fabulous life as a concert pianist. So, when she reached the age of 16, she packed her luggage and headed to Paris, France, to study classical music and singing. Finally, she had her first taste of freedom. Little did she know that she had also taken her first step toward fame and fortune.

Unfortunately, Agatha had a problem. Every time she took to the stage, perched on the piano stool, and tried to perform, stage fright would take hold. She would get terribly flustered. Poor Agatha even had nightmares about her piano breaking or the keys sticking together.

With her grand plans of becoming a musician seemingly dashed, Agatha needed a new plan. So, she picked up her pen and, a safe distance from any

stages, began to write. And once she started, she couldn't stop. Wonderful words, poems, and stories flowed onto the page.

Agatha thought this was it. Surely, there would be a scramble for her book of poems, and publishers would argue over her! But sadly not. The publishers were unconvinced by Agatha's poetic genius. She was disheartened, but she did not give up. Writing was her passion, after all.

Agatha ditched poetry and turned her attention to something decidedly more dramatic: writing a novel called *The Mysterious Affair at Styles*. It was rejected by publishers six times, but she would not accept defeat, and eventually, she secured a deal. Phew. Finally!

Agatha secured her status as the queen of crime stories by writing "whodunit" tales about two detectives, Hercule Poirot and Miss Marple. They investigated all manner of murders and mysteries and cleared up numerous dastardly crimes. During her career, Agatha wrote more than 60 of these detective books, including her most celebrated stories, *Murder on the Orient Express* and *The Mystery of the Blue Train*.

Wherever Agatha went, she was a quiet observer, immersing herself in the culture, the language, and the people. She listened carefully and soaked everything up. When it comes to being a detective, or even writing about detectives, attention to detail is important. It's what solves crimes!

Even though Agatha had wanted success, it turned out that being famous was rather uncomfortable and irksome for her. She preferred to live a quiet life and didn't want to be in the public eye like other celebrities. She loathed loud parties, dodged press interviews, and avoided speaking or appearing in public. She even refused to have her photograph on the cover of her books! Agatha also agreed to become the president of the world-famous Detection Club—a club for crime writers—but only if she never had to give any talks or speeches.

Agatha kept such a low profile that when she was invited to be the guest of honor at a party at The Savoy Hotel in London, the doorman did not recognize her and refused to let her in! Agatha was too shy to make a fuss, so she slinked off into the night and returned home to bed.

And then, one day, Agatha disappeared into thin air. For 11 long days, the famous author completely vanished, with no clues to her whereabouts. What a conundrum! The newspapers were filled with feverish theories. Perhaps she had been kidnapped? Abducted by aliens? Or maybe she had been on a runaway train when it flew off the edge of a cliff?

Agatha was eventually discovered at a luxury spa. She was completely unbothered by the ruckus she'd caused and gave no explanation of her whereabouts!

From then on, Agatha resolved to travel as much as she could and have as many adventures as possible. She voyaged all over the world to South Africa, Australia, New Zealand, Hawaii, and Canada. She adored swimming in the sea and was one of the first English women to learn to surf! Everywhere she went, she took her trusty —and rather hefty—typewriter so she could work on her latest novel.

Today, Agatha Christie is remembered as one of the greatest authors of all time. Her books have been translated into over 100 languages, which is more than any other writer. In total, she has sold more than two billion books. Phenomenal!

David Bowie

(1947–2016)

David Jones lived an ordinary life in a normal part of London with his normal family, until one day his big brother Terry sent him some music records. All alone in his bedroom, David slid the vinyl discs out of their sleeves and, one by one, put them on the record player. As the music played and the sound filled the air, David jumped around. The shy, self-conscious kid let loose and wiggled his hips! Something magical had happened—David had discovered rock and roll, and it was magnificent!

When David's father realized that his shy son liked music, he saw a chance to hang out with him and have fun. He started taking David to see bands at local venues. Watching amazing artists in the flesh, like Fats Domino, Little Richard, and even Elvis Presley, rocked David's world.

His life was changed forever. Inspired by what he had heard, David learned to play the piano and the ukulele (which is a bit like a small guitar). Then, with dreams of stardom, he gathered some friends together and formed a band. But David still felt average and dull. If only he could be different somehow.

And then, by a twist of fate, David fell out with his friend George over a girl they both liked. They had a fist fight, and George injured David's eye. Ouch! David was livid and in pain! He went to a special eye hospital to get it checked out and discovered that his eye had been damaged. From now on, his eyes would be different colors, and one of his pupils would always appear larger than the other. Luckily for George, David grew to like this new feature. He now had very different eyes to other people and was unique!

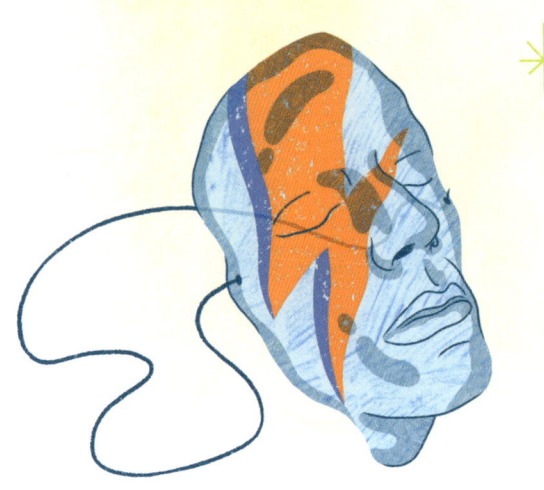

"Maybe the route to being brave is not pretending to be something you're not. Perhaps it's about finding a way to face the world exactly as you are."

However, having interesting eyes would only take David so far. He still needed to find an identity as a musician. David wasn't sure who he wanted to be—he just knew he wanted to stand out and be different. So, he grew his hair long and changed his name to David Bowie, who sounded more rock and roll than David Jones. He also tried various different types of music until he discovered what worked for him.

David also knew that he needed to bring star quality to his performances on stage. It was one thing to leap about in his bedroom, but connecting with an audience at a concert was another matter altogether. He was a quiet person and felt self-conscious when people were watching him. Nerves would kick in, and David would stand there, frozen to the spot. He had so much to say through his music, but at this rate, nobody would ever hear his voice.

So, David came up with an idea. He would become exuberantly theatrical on stage! He created characters, such as Ziggy Stardust, and dyed his hair bright red. David also wore sparkly outfits, platform boots, skin-tight jumpsuits, and showstopping makeup. When he was Ziggy, David could put on a flamboyant disguise. He became someone else entirely and felt free to express himself without fear. He sang and performed dazzling and dramatic sets. David was energetic and exciting—people couldn't take their eyes off him.

At first, when David's shows were over and he stepped off stage, he would go back to being shy and reserved. But switching back and forth got really confusing, and he kind of forgot how to be his authentic self. He felt like the characters he had created were taking over, and he didn't like it. He needed to find a way to be himself.

One day in London, David met a shy young fan. He knew what it was like to let shyness hold you back, so he sat down and had a long chat with the boy. He told him about his new invisible, magical mask. David explained that without the mask, he felt nervous and awkward in all kinds of situations. He said that wearing the mask made him feel much better and gave him the courage to face the world. He pretended to take the invisible mask off his face, handed it to the boy and told him to put it on. Now he had a magic mask, too!

David pretended to make another mask from thin air and placed it over his own face. He smiled, looking relaxed and happy. They both wore invisible masks, so nobody would know they were wearing them. They both felt safer and more able to do brave things.

Maybe the route to being brave is not pretending to be something you're not. Perhaps it's about finding a way to face the world exactly as you are.

BE TRUE TO YOU

Quiet Reflection

Use these prompts to help you work out what makes you unique. Don't be afraid to ask friends or family if you need help working out why you are so special!

If I were an animal, I would be a . . .

My friends and family would describe me as . . .

One of my greatest strengths is . . .

I am a good friend because . . .

The nicest things people say about me are . . .

I am special because . . .

I like myself because . . .

10 things I am good at are . . .

I am strong because I have . . .

I am proud of myself for . . .

FIND YOUR PEOPLE

Alan Turing
(1912–1954)

When famous mathematician and computer scientist Alan Turing was little, his parents moved abroad. They traveled to India for his father's work when he was two years old, leaving Alan and his older brother behind. Alan didn't understand why they had left—was something wrong with him? Had he done something bad? Alan felt lost and confused.

Alan's parents didn't want to leave their boys behind, but they worried that the journey would be dangerous or the children might get sick. They made the difficult decision to leave them in England with a foster family called the Wards, an older couple who lived by the sea.

Alan's world had been tipped upside down. He was living with strange people in a strange place. His parents would come back to visit every few years, but that was not enough! When his brother went away to boarding school, it was the final straw. Alan was so sad. He withdrew even further into his own little world. None of this made any sense to him.

Numbers, on the other hand, did make sense to Alan. He loved the sequences and patterns of mathematics. At school, his teacher noticed that Alan could solve difficult problems that others couldn't. In fact, he didn't just solve them; he whizzed through them!

Alan felt comfortable around numbers but not so much around people. Other people were complicated, strange, and perplexing. The other children thought Alan was unusual, so they teased him. Alan felt like he had to hide parts of himself from the other children—his intellect, his mathematical skills, and even his sexuality. (Unfortunately, when Alan Turing was alive, being gay

was illegal!) This made making friends seem like an impossibility. Machines were much easier to understand.

By the time he went to the University of Cambridge, England, to study mathematics, it was clear that the kids in his school had been right—Alan was anything but normal. Alan was a mathematical genius!

You'd think that being a mathematical marvel would make Alan want to show off. Even though his work was incredible, and he could solve super complicated sums, he struggled to speak in front of people. During debates and discussions, he would sit in silence.

One day, Alan was asked to present his work on a complex problem. He became so nervous and overwhelmed that he could not say a word and sat silently in front of the group for several minutes. Eventually, another student had to step in and present his work on Alan's behalf. Alan was so embarrassed, that his confidence seemed to dissolve into a puddle on the floor.

Alan's air of awkwardness and embarrassment did not make him a likely superhero. He had an aversion to eye contact, a jittery voice, and crumpled clothes. But, when World War II started in 1939, the British Secret Service called on Alan to help them defeat Germany. They needed his brain to help them win the war against Adolf Hitler, leader of the Nazis, a group that killed six million Jews (as well as thousands of other people, such as gay and disabled people).

Alan was recruited alongside other mathematicians to work on a secret project at an English estate called Bletchley Park. Their job was to decipher the codes produced by the Enigma machine, a complicated device used by the Nazis to transmit secret messages.

Alan and his team worked day and night for six months to decipher the patterns in the German codes. It was

tremendously tricky as the coding system changed daily. Knowing that the lives of millions of people depended on him was a lot of pressure, but together with his team of codebreakers, Alan was in his element. He helped invent a codebreaking machine called the Bombe, which could work things out faster than humans.

Alan was highly respected by his colleagues. They were in awe of his intellect and liked his eccentricities. They giggled when he chained his mug to the radiator so nobody could steal it, and they chuckled when he wore a gas mask while cycling to protect him from hay fever. And they were amazed when they discovered how fast he could run. Alan would zoom off and run the 40 miles to London for a meeting.

Finally, Alan had found his people! They respected and understood him. And Alan felt comfortable and confident when he was with them. His codebreaking colleagues became his friends. They knew he was gay, and they liked him just the way he was. He was proud of being different.

In 1940, after months of hard work, the codebreakers figured out the secret code and deciphered the contents of 178 messages. Once they had done that, they were able to build lots more Bombe machines and solve all the other codes. The Germans did not stand a chance. Alan's work helped to shorten World War II by two years and helped save over two million lives!

After the war, Alan was arrested for being in a relationship with a man. Sadly, the last years of his life were unfortunate and lonely. The government eventually apologized to Alan for the hurt and damage they had caused, but it was too little too late.

Alan Turing was a genius and a superhero. The machine he created is one of the first computing devices ever built, making Alan the founding father of computer science. Every time you use a computer to play a game, message someone, or watch a video, you can do so because of Alan Turing's work.

Yao Ming
(born 1980)

Yao just wanted to blend in with the crowd. However, by the time he was 11 years old, he was already 6ft 5in tall! He towered over the other children and most of the adults too. Being so tall and so quiet meant people struggled to hear him when he spoke. Sometimes, he would stutter when he was nervous, making it even harder for him to communicate. He often felt like he was living up in the clouds or in a different world. If only he could be like everybody else!

Basketball was in Yao's family. Both of his parents were professional basketball players in China. They encouraged Yao to play even though, at first, he wasn't interested. He much preferred table tennis, and the last thing he wanted to do was follow in his parent's giant footsteps.

And then one day, his mother took him to watch the world-famous Harlem Globetrotters play basketball. He loved seeing the tall players use their height as a strength. Plus, they seemed to be having a lot of fun!

Yao began to play some basketball and was soon recruited by a sports academy in Beijing, China. Although it was incredibly competitive, his talent was evident. The coaches were amazed at his speed and agility.

By the time he was fully grown, Yao was 7ft 6in, which was perfect for professional basketball. Even though he was tall, he didn't want to simply stand by the hoop and drop the ball in. Instead, he worked on refining all his basketball skills, including dribbling, shooting, and handling the ball. That way, he could play like someone of average height but with the advantage of being so tall.

One day, a scout from the Shanghai Sharks spotted Yao and snapped him up for their team. He became their shining star player and took the Sharks to victory in the championships. He scored loads of hoops and made winning look easy.

In 2002, Yao was just starting to feel comfortable when he was offered the opportunity to join the American NBA and play for the Houston Rockets. Yao was worried about going to the USA for lots of reasons. He was concerned about making mistakes and letting his teammates down. He also thought people would think he was too tall—he would be the tallest player in the whole league! Yao was even worried about making friends and the fact that he could not speak English very well. Moving to another country was scary.

Yao's life changed forever when he landed. He was taken aback by a huge crowd of photographers that had come to greet him. Their cameras flashed brightly in his face—they all wanted a picture of him. From that day on, Yao was followed and swamped by press and photographers. Yao did not like all this attention. He was tempted to turn around and get straight back on the plane. Instead, he took a deep breath and tried to smile politely.

In the USA, everything seemed strange and unfamiliar—the cars, the food, and the language. All he wanted to do was hide away in his hotel room. At first, he had help from a translator, but he found it hard to speak English when he was out shopping or in a restaurant on his own. During his first television interview, he was asked all kinds of questions, but Yao could not say a word. It was very awkward for him.

Yao was incredibly shy when he first met his teammates, too. He felt like an alien from another planet! Luckily, they were extremely welcoming. They were happy and excited that he was joining them, so they hugged him and told him not to worry. His teammates took him out to play golf, introduced him to people, and showed him around. They even brought in a Chinese teacher to teach them about China and Chinese traditions. And when it was Chinese New Year, they organized a party for him to celebrate with his friends. Gradually, Yao started to feel more settled. He even discovered various things about America that he loved, like pizza, ribs, computer games, action movies, and huge cars that he could fit into!

When it came to basketball, Yao didn't need words. His team understood him on the court, and they loved him for his skills, towering presence, and calm, kind personality, even under pressure. Being part of the team really helped Yao. They made him feel safe like he belonged.

Yao played for the Rockets for nine seasons and blazed a trail for Chinese players to play basketball in the USA. He became a massive superstar. One day, he was walking along the street when he saw his face on a giant billboard. He was so embarrassed! But then he realized that the thing he felt shy about had become his strength. He was with people who loved him for who he was. If he had disappeared into the background, he would not have been given the opportunity to travel around the world playing the sport he loved with his friends.

USA FRESH PIZZA

PIZZA PIZZA PIZZA

AMERICAN HOT PIZZA

E DELICIOUS PIZZA

FRESH HOT PIZZA

Soda

Misty Copeland
(born 1982)

Misty lived with her mother and five brothers and sisters, all squished together in one motel room on the side of a busy road in California, USA. Her father was not around, and though her mother tried her best to look after everyone, there wasn't enough money or food.

If she wasn't at home with her family, Misty was extremely shy. She found it hard to talk to people. When she was feeling lonely, anxious, or something big was happening, writing in her journal gave her a way to express her emotions. At school, Misty did not like people looking at her. She would hide quietly at the back of the room to avoid being the center of attention.

One day, when Misty was 13 years old, she was messing around on the basketball court with her brothers and sisters. Cindy, a local ballet teacher, spotted them and suggested Misty join in with her ballet class. Misty had never seen a Black ballerina, so she wasn't convinced. Plus, she was in her scruffy clothes and giant sports socks, so she wasn't dressed for the occasion!

Trying new things was scary for Misty, and she was worried about being with a bunch of people she didn't know. Instead of joining in, she sat on a bench and watched from the sidelines.

And so it continued. Every week, Misty sat on the bench and observed the class. She watched closely, taking in every little detail. Then, one day, she finally found the courage to stand up, step forward, and join in.

Everyone knew more than her! Misty tried to follow along, but she felt incredibly nervous and worried about the mistakes she would undoubtedly

make. But Cindy encouraged Misty and helped her point her toes correctly and get into the different positions.

Misty was tiny but very strong, with long, flexible legs. Cindy noticed there was something special about the way Misty held her body and the way she moved around with elegance and grace. Cindy told Misty she thought she could be a brilliant professional ballet dancer. Misty giggled. She did not believe a word of it.

Misty continued with ballet, intrigued to see where it might lead her. After just a couple of months, Misty had mastered dancing *en pointe*—on the tip of her toes—something that most ballerinas take years to master. She went to class five days a week, working incredibly hard. Ballet became more than just a hobby for Misty. It was a way to express and challenge herself. When she danced, she felt special. Just a few years later, Misty won an award and a scholarship to attend a special ballet school.

Despite her undeniable talent, Misty was still very shy and often doubted herself. She would feel nervous before performances and fretted about making a mistake. Misty worried that people would not accept her for the

"Misty acted as her own softly spoken cheerleader. When she had doubts, she would tell herself she was strong and beautiful and that she could do this!"

way she looked or the way she danced. Sometimes, she even hid behind the other dancers! Step by step, after a few shows, she felt more comfortable and was able to step out and shine. It turns out she just needed to warm up a little.

Misty acted as her own softly spoken cheerleader. When she had doubts, she would tell herself she was strong and beautiful and that she could do this! She imagined herself performing magnificently while the audience clapped and cheered. By the time she stepped onto the stage, she knew everything would be perfect.

But something was bothering Misty. She had never met a ballerina who looked like her. Not one. They didn't even make ballet shoes to match her skin color. Deep down, Misty felt like an outsider in the world of ballet. Then, one day, she heard about another African American ballerina called Raven Wilkinson. Misty was delighted to discover that Raven knew who she was! Now an old lady, she had been following Misty's career all along. The two dancers met up and became great friends. Finally, having a role model to inspire and motivate her helped Misty become the best ballerina she could be.

In 2015, Misty became the first-ever African American principal dancer at the American Ballet Theatre, one of the world's most famous classical ballet companies. She won all kinds of awards and became the lead dancer in *The Nutcracker*, *Swan Lake*, and *Romeo and Juliet*. It turned out that Misty's teacher was right all along. Little Misty had transformed into the most incredible ballet dancer.

Yves Saint Laurent

(1936–2008)

Little Yves watched his mother sashay down the stairs in her new dress. She swished the fabric and flipped her hair. Usually, Yves loved to see his mother's latest looks, but this one was so horrible that he burst into tears!

Yves was an extremely shy, reserved, and sensitive young boy. To escape the reality of being an outcast at school and avoid social interactions outside his family, Yves escaped into a fantasy of becoming a fashion designer. At the young age of three, his young mind was already filled with dreams, designs, and beauty. He had a strong eye for color and was adamant that his mother's dress did not look good on her, so she changed her outfit to keep him happy.

Yves lived in a stylish townhouse in Oran, Algeria, with his parents and two younger sisters. His father was a successful businessman who owned a chain of movie theaters, so the family was lucky enough to have plenty of money. Their world was filled with bright colors, sunshine, and people from different cultures. From a young age, Yves was immersed in sophisticated society.

His mother spent her days sipping tea, fanning herself, and discussing fashion and theater with other ladies. She loved dressing up each evening for dinner and going out to parties. As Yves grew up, he was passionate about fashion and would pore over his mum's magazines, taking in all the beautiful designs.

Sadly, Yves' life at school wasn't so happy. The other children made fun of him and pushed him around for being sensitive, effeminate, and different from the other children. Yves did not feel safe and often missed school, becoming even more nervous and fragile.

To escape his pain, Yves would close his eyes and let his imagination fill with vibrant pictures of dramatic dresses and ornate costumes. In his world of fabric and color, he was free to be his own unique self. Even as a child, he understood that clothes have the power to change how we feel about ourselves.

When he was 14 years old, his mother took him to the theater as a special treat. The set and the costumes had been designed by a famous artist, and Yves was so blown away by their beauty that tears rolled down his cheeks.

Back at home, Yves decided to make his own miniature theater. Using crates and bits of wood, he made the stage, an elaborate sign, and tiny little lights. He created hundreds of intricate costumes for the cardboard figures, carefully selecting the colors and fabric combinations. Each figure had a wardrobe of different costumes, all crafted from snippets of material that his mother gave him. Family members received ornate invitations to come watch his entertaining shows.

Gradually, Yves progressed from making paper dolls to sewing dresses for

his sisters and mother. His ideas were finally coming to life! When Yves entered a fashion design competition in Paris, France, he won third prize. The following year, he entered again, and this time, he won first prize.

Inspired by his success, Yves traveled to Paris, France, where he was introduced to the editor-in-chief of *Vogue* magazine. The editor agreed to mentor Yves and encouraged him to study to become a fashion designer.

"Yves' soulful sensitivity was his superpower. It allowed him to create game-changing garments that made his customers feel powerful."

Later, Christian Dior—the well-known, celebrated designer—was so impressed by Yves' talent that he hired him on the spot. Even though he flourished in his new position, Yves was in awe of his new boss and found it difficult to speak to him. To help him feel fiercer and more fabulous, he turned to fashion. Yves wore closely fitted jackets that were neatly buttoned up like a suit of armor to give him the feeling of protection.

Yves channeled all his passion and emotions into his work, but the fashion world was noisy, and he was still shy and softly spoken. He struggled to socialize at the glittering parties, often stuttering and suffering with nerves. He preferred to spend time with the people who understood and loved him just the way he was.

When Christian died a few years later, Yves was asked to become head designer at Dior. Yves took the promotion in his stride and won many awards, building a loyal following of admirers. Then, in 1961, Yves' ultimate dream came true. He launched his own fashion label: Yves Saint Laurent.

Yves remained humble, modest, and uninterested in fame throughout his career. He preferred to hide behind the curtains at his fashion shows and let his designs do the talking. He would only come out on the runway reluctantly if someone gave him a gentle shove.

Yves' soulful sensitivity was his superpower. It allowed him to create game-changing garments that made his customers feel powerful. Fashion gave Yves the freedom to be himself, and in turn, his designs helped others express themselves. His glamorous suits, dresses, blazers, jumpsuits, and shirts took over the world!

FIND YOUR PEOPLE

Quiet Reflection

The people we choose to spend time with make a huge difference in how we feel and how confident we are! Answer these questions to help you find your people.

I feel loved and supported by . . .

I learn the most from . . .

I have the most fun when I spend time with . . .

I have the most interesting conversations with . . .

I have lots in common with . . .

I feel like I belong when I am with . . .

When I have a problem, I like to talk to . . .

I am a good friend because . . .

I would like to be friends with . . .

The first step I could take toward building that friendship is . . .

BE A BIT BRAVER

Billie Eilish

(born 2001)

When Billie Eilish Pirate Baird O'Connell was at home with her parents and her big brother Finneas, she felt safe. But when she wasn't in their cozy bungalow in Los Angeles, USA, she struggled—even though her middle name was Pirate, she didn't feel much like a pirate at all!

Billie feared so many things, including the dark and being alone. When she was away from her parents, she would worry that something terrible might happen to them. Billie and her family slept in one big bed until she was 11 years old, all snuggled up together. If she woke up in the night and her parents weren't there, she would panic until they came to comfort her. When she was older, instead of going out with her friends or going to parties, she would stay at home in their little house. That's where she felt safe.

Billie's parents were very creative people who encouraged Billie and her brother to sing, dance, and play musical instruments. Billie listened to all kinds of music and learned to play the piano and the ukulele. She sang in a choir and spent hours writing original songs with Finneas. Her parents encouraged creativity so much that they allowed the children to go to bed whenever they wanted, if they were making, writing, or singing music. If Billie was in the middle of writing a song, she was allowed to stay up all night to finish it. Imagine!

Billie would dance for hours and hours every single day. She found that when she was dancing, she didn't feel afraid or alone. Instead, she felt powerful and free. Billie dreamed of being a dancer so that she could dance all the time. But then, when she was 13 years old, she injured her hip badly and had to stop dancing forever. Billie was heartbroken.

To cheer her up and distract her from her injury, Billie's dance teacher asked her and Finneas to record a song for the upcoming dance show. At first, Billie wasn't sure, but then she decided to pivot like a dancer and focus on making music.

So, Billie and Finneas set to work. Finneas had already written a gorgeous song called "Ocean Eyes" and asked Billie to record it with him. For hours and hours, days and days, they worked on it in their bedroom, sitting together on the edge of the bed. They recorded different sounds and melodies, harnessing the beauty of Billie's glorious voice. And when they were done, they sat back and grinned. They knew they had created something precious and perfect.

Billie and Finneas uploaded their song to a music-sharing platform so that their dance teacher could listen and begin choreographing a superb dance performance. They headed to bed without thinking much more about it, but then a funny thing happened!

While they were sleeping, hundreds of people downloaded the song. And then thousands. And then hundreds of thousands. The song they had recorded in their bedroom had gone viral! Billie couldn't believe it. Her dreams were coming true—she was going to be a musician. People were listening to and loving her music. The invitations soon started rolling in. People everywhere wanted Billie to perform for them on television and the radio.

Billie wanted to make music and share it with the world, but she was afraid. Recording a song with her brother in her bedroom was one thing, but the thought of stepping on stage as a solo artist petrified her. She could just about manage singing in a choir if she was surrounded by other

people, but the idea of singing alone was too much!

However, Billie saw that she was allowing her fears to control and silence her. Unless she changed her way of thinking, she would miss her big moment. So, Billie made an important decision—she would be more like a pirate! After all, pirates don't hide away at home—they sail the seven seas! They don't follow the rules or allow their fears to control them. Shiver me timbers!

Billie's family worked together to create the conditions that Billie needed to perform. It was all hands on deck! They did everything they could to help Billie feel safe on stage, including choosing the right curtains, lights, seating, and microphone. Finneas promised he would be by her side every step of the way, whether they were writing or performing. If Billie had a wobble and worried that she wasn't good enough, Finneas would give her a pep talk.

Billie remembered that pirates don't care what people think of them. They are not easily intimidated and do what they want. They're swashbucklers! Billie resolved to be the same. If she wanted to wear big baggy clothes and color her hair green, she would! She'd wear whatever made her feel good and say what was on her mind.

Billie sings about things that are important to her, including the things she's experienced and the fears she has faced. Being open and honest helps her feel brave and confident. Billie also helps her fans talk about their feelings. In her song, "Come Out and Play", Billie sings about supporting someone who is softly spoken and hiding themselves away. She urges them to come out and play so that they can share their talent with the world. Perhaps she wrote it for herself, or perhaps she wrote it for you.

Maya Gabeira
(born 1987)

Little Maya was in and out of hospital with asthma, a condition that affects the airways that carry air in and out of the lungs. Whenever she had a cold, she would struggle to breathe, and her strength would be zapped. She was pretty fragile, so everyone told her she had to be very careful.

Isolated and alone, shy little Maya was missing out on so much. Her sister had lots of friends and could go to sleepovers or to camp, but Maya had to stay at home. Spending so much time alone made Maya feel even more shy.

Maya lived by the sea in Rio de Janeiro, Brazil, with opportunity and adventure on her doorstep. But Maya was stuck inside, her nose pressed against the window, gazing longingly at the ocean. As the waves crashed and the tide inched closer, Maya was sure she could hear the sea calling to her.

Noticing that her asthma had improved a little, Maya's doctor encouraged her to exercise and get fresh air. It was time for Maya to strengthen her lungs and build her courage! Her parents signed her up to the local surf school.

At first, Maya was like a fish out of water. She wasn't used to being around other people, and she was terrible at surfing! The other kids could ride the waves, but Maya struggled to even stand on the board. Maya did not care, nor did she get frustrated. In fact, she could not stop grinning. For the first time in her life, she felt free. Besides, Maya was used to difficulties. She kept practicing until, after one month, she finally stood up on the board.

Maya soon progressed to riding tiny little waves; gradually moving to the open water. Soon, she was confident enough to try the foamy waves

> *"Maya felt like giving up, but she told herself that life isn't supposed to be easy—failing is part of the journey. You must learn to pick yourself up, learn from your mistakes, and try again."*

that crashed onto the shore. These waves were bigger than Maya! Even though it was scary, Maya ignored her fears and told herself to be brave. She reminded herself that being afraid is part of life.

When the waves near her house were no longer a challenge, Maya knew it was time for her to search for the largest waves she could find. She was scared to leave home all on her own and be around people she didn't know, but again, Maya confronted her fears. She told herself she deserved to follow her dreams, so she packed her bags and hugged her mother and father goodbye. Maya headed to Australia and Hawaii to search for the most epic waves.

Maya trained and trained to become the best. She gave it her all despite being wiped out and falling into the sea repeatedly. She'd simply grab hold of her board, swim back to shore, and try again.

Eventually, Maya was ready to conquer the biggest, tallest, most dangerous waves. She moved to Nazare, Portugal, home to the world's largest waves. There, she studied and observed the sea and the wave patterns. She took her time, breathing in the sea and tuning into the spirit of the waves she planned to tackle.

Then, the day Maya had been waiting for arrived. She was ready. She took to the water, focusing only on the wave and the task ahead. However, things did not go to plan. Maya started off well, but as the wave loomed over her, it overpowered her and knocked her off her board. It was a total wipeout.

Water weighing as much as a blue whale crashed onto Maya and plunged her into the depths below.

Brave Maya told herself not to panic. As she fought for her breath, time seemed to slow down. She was used to staying calm when it felt as though there was no air in her lungs due to her asthma. Deep down in the sea, she marveled at how her supposed weakness was now a strength.

Maya nearly drowned and was rushed to hospital in need of lots of operations. She stayed there for a long time, and her recovery was difficult. Maya felt like giving up, but she told herself that life isn't supposed to be easy—failing is part of the journey. You must learn to pick yourself up, learn from your mistakes, and try again.

So, when Maya felt better, she got back on her surfboard. How brave is that? Then, seven years after the accident, she conquered a wave that measured 73.5ft tall—the biggest wave anyone, anywhere, had ever surfed. She'd done it! She'd mastered the monster wave and, in doing so, had squashed her fears.

Ashley Fiolek

(born 1990)

Ashley and her mother, Roni, were in the kitchen one day when a pile of pots and pans toppled from the worktop and clattered to the ground. Roni leaped into the air with a loud squeal, but her three-year-old daughter did not scream. In fact, she did not move a muscle.

Ashley's mother was confused. Why didn't Ashley react to the loud crash? To try and get Ashley's attention, Roni bashed the pans together like drums. Still, little Ashley did not flinch—she didn't even look up! At that moment, Roni realized that her quiet little girl couldn't hear her. Later that week, a doctor confirmed what she suspected: Ashley was deaf. Now her parents understood why she hadn't started speaking.

To help their daughter, Ashley's parents started learning sign language and joined sports teams, dance classes, and community groups for deaf people. They didn't want Ashley to feel like she was different—they wanted her to know that she belonged.

Despite her parents' best efforts, Ashley often felt left out and lonely. Communicating with the other children was extremely challenging, and she struggled to fit in and make friends. Some kids were even cruel and made fun of her. Ashley withdrew into her shell, spending most of her time alone.

Now, Ashley's parents loved motorcycles. They competed in races sometimes and would take Ashley to watch. One day, they wondered if riding a bike might help Ashley feel more confident, so they took her for a ride when she was just three years old—that's when everything changed!

Even though she was young, Ashley wasn't scared at all. In fact, as she sat on the motorcycle, with its powerful engine underneath her, she felt fearless. She adored the power of the engine, the spinning wheels, and speeding round corners. It was thrilling, and Ashley felt invincible! Riding on a motorcycle can sometimes be dangerous, but she loved it.

It didn't matter that she was smaller than everyone else at the track, that she was deaf, or that she was the only girl. Finally, Ashley felt like she was the same as everyone else—she belonged. When she was riding motocross (off-road motorcycle racing), she felt free! Ashley loved it so much that when night fell, and it was time to go home, she would burst into tears.

When Ashley was old enough, she wanted to enter races herself, but some people thought it was too dangerous for her to drive a powerful vehicle. If she couldn't hear the engines, how would she know when to change gear? And how would she know if the other riders were approaching?

But they needn't have worried. Ashley might not have been able to hear the roaring engines, but she could feel their vibrations. Rather than relying on hearing the bikes, she carefully scanned her surroundings. Without all the distracting noise, Ashley could race in a calm, stress-free state. Plus, she would usually get so far ahead of the other competitors that it didn't matter whether she could hear them or not!

"Ashley shows us that taking risks might seem scary and uncomfortable at first, but if you just stay home where it is safe, you'll never know what you are capable of."

Ashley did have one rather significant problem, though. She would get so nervous before a big race that she would be sick. Luckily, once she was on the bike, she could hold it together and focus on the race. Throwing up while wearing a helmet would have been revolting!

Ashley felt rather invincible when she was on her bike, but away from the track, her shyness would still take over. If people tried to talk to her, she would avoid eye contact or hide completely. At the age of 16, Ashley won her first national championship, but during the victory interview, she was so nervous that she froze.

Even though Ashley is shy, she is incredibly brave. Motocross is extremely dangerous! She has fallen off her motorcycle many times and has broken bones and teeth. One time, she snapped her collarbone in two. But even though she was in agony, she didn't quit. She simply wiggled her fingers and toes, hopped back on her bike, and crossed the finish line to win the championship.

Ashley shows us that taking risks might seem scary and uncomfortable at first, but if you just stay home where it is safe, you'll never know what you are capable of.

Phiona Mutesi
(born 1996)

Phiona lived in an impoverished part of Katwe in Uganda, Africa, in a one-room dwelling with no windows and a leaky tin roof. There was no bathroom, sofa, or fancy furniture, just two mattresses on the floor, a copy of the Bible, and a pot for washing.

It was a dirty and difficult place to live, with heaps of litter, polluted water, and stray animals scavenging for food. When the regular floods came to the area, sewage water would wash through the slum, bringing sickness and destruction. People would regularly be forced to clamber onto their rooftops to avoid being washed away. They worried about finding food, protecting themselves from thieves, their homes collapsing, and illness spreading. Lots of people died here due to the terrible conditions, including Phiona's father and sister. They passed away when she was just a toddler.

When Phiona was nine years old, she had to stop attending school because it was too expensive, and her mother needed her to work to help support the family. Instead of going to a classroom, Phiona spent her days selling maize in the street with her brother and foraging for food.

Phiona felt trapped. She daringly dreamed of a different life but did not know how to make it happen. She also did not know how to talk about her feelings as she was far too focused on finding food and simply surviving. Phiona felt very small indeed—and so did her world.

One day, Phiona and her brother searched high and low for food. They were exhausted and hungry when they stumbled upon an old, unused church with a broken roof. Phiona prayed to find food. Perhaps someone inside had something they could eat? Holding her breath, she squinted through a gap in the door.

At first, Phiona did not understand what she was seeing. A group of smiling kids sat in silence, looking down at square chequered boards with black and white figurines. Phiona had never seen anyone play chess before, so she was spellbound. Chess isn't commonly played in Uganda. There isn't even a word for it in Swahili, the national language.

On the other side of the door lay an opportunity for Phiona to try something new. She needed to summon the courage to step toward it, but she just stood there. Luckily, the organizer, a man called Robert, saw Phiona and invited her and her brother inside. He gave them some oats and asked a four-year-old girl named Gloria to show Phiona the chess pieces.

Phiona was obsessed. From that day forward, when she wasn't working or sleeping, she was at the club playing chess. She had to travel miles and miles in the roasting sunshine to get there. Even though she couldn't read or write, chess helped Phiona realize she was super smart. She loved solving the puzzles that the pieces presented and setting traps for her opponent.

Phiona realized that chess was a lot like life in the slum. It was about staying safe from danger, solving problems, and looking after your family. No matter how many challenges she faced, chess remained constant. The chess pieces were always there for her. When she played chess, she was the boss. She placed the pieces wherever she decided. She was in charge.

Phiona was obsessed with winning at first, yet she soon discovered that if you think only of victory, it clouds your judgment, and you make silly mistakes. Gradually, Phiona became a calmer, more deep-thinking player, one who waits for their opponent to make a mistake and then leaps! By the time she was 11 years old, Phiona had become Uganda's national junior girls' champion. The top player among all the girls in the whole country!

With two other kids from her chess club, she was chosen to represent her country at Africa's International Children's Chess Tournament in Sudan. It was the first time Phiona had ever left the slum, let alone been on a plane.

She was so nervous. A world of opportunity lay ahead of her; she just needed the courage to step forward. Phiona took a deep breath and boarded the plane just like on the day she entered the church for the first time and discovered chess. As the aircraft rose in the sky and pushed through the clouds, Phiona thought she had gone to heaven! When she arrived at her hotel, with her own bed, a beautiful bathroom, and room service, Phiona felt like a real-life queen.

Even though Phiona and her team were much younger than the other competitors, they won the championship. When they arrived back in Katwe, people cheered and celebrated their new local heroes.

Phenomenal Phiona became the first Ugandan woman to earn a chess title. She went to university, traveled all over the world, and now lives and works for a big company in the USA. It just goes to show that sometimes, taking a little step into the unknown—even if you're afraid—can lead to all kinds of wonderful things.

BE A BIT BRAVER

Quiet Reflection

The people in this chapter were able to accomplish great things because they stepped outside of their comfort zone and found their courage. Finish these sentences to help you work out how you can be more confident in your life.

But now I can do it because . . .

When I stand up tall, with my shoulders back
and my head held high, I feel . . .

If I was not afraid, I would . . .

The thing that stops me from being brave is . . .

If I don't try to be a little bit braver, I will feel . . .

I remember a time when I took brave action.
It made me feel . . .

I have been putting off . . .

The first step I could take is . . .

TAKE A STAND

Marcus Rashford
(born 1997)

It was time for Marcus to go to bed, but he was very hungry. There was no food in the house—not even a loaf of bread. He had been at school all day and then out on the street playing football for hours, and now he was starving. He figured that he could go to sleep, and when he woke up, he would feel better, and he could get something to eat at school.

Marcus lived in a run-down part of Manchester, England, with his mother, two older brothers, and two older sisters. His mother was not at home much because she had three jobs. She worked as a cashier in the day, a cleaner at night, and a kitchen porter at weekends. Life was a struggle. No matter what she did or how hard she worked, there was never enough money or food to go around. Sometimes, they would visit food banks and soup kitchens to have something to eat, and sometimes, local store owners gave Marcus leftover food. Marcus did not tell anyone what life was like at home. He kept it to himself.

Marcus was a very shy, quiet boy. At school, his worst nightmare was being asked to read out loud in class. Fear and awkwardness made him stumble over his words, and then he would feel ashamed, which made it even worse.

But when he played soccer, Marcus could forget about his troubles. He dreamed of playing professionally for Manchester United so that he could look after his mother, pay for her to go on vacation, and buy her a big house in a nice part of town.

Marcus played a lot of soccer outside on the street, but he kept smashing roof tiles and garbage bins. To save the neighborhood from destruction,

his mother signed him up for a local team when he was five years old. His time there was short-lived. Marcus' soccer abilities were spotted by the youth scouts of Manchester United, and he was invited to join the club's academy when he was just seven years old.

Marcus loved it! But, traveling there and back so many times a week was getting expensive. Sometimes, he would miss training because he could not pay for the tickets. His coaches noticed what was going on and helped him by finding people who could drive Marcus to and from training.

Then, when Marcus was 11 years old, his mum made a difficult decision. Worried that she could not look after him properly, she signed Marcus up to go and live in the soccer club's accommodation. If Marcus wanted to play soccer professionally, there was no other choice. Although the club was just an hour up the road, and he could visit at weekends, Marcus missed his family heaps. He even missed wrestling with his brother!

Life at the academy was pressurized and competitive. It was a far cry from street soccer, with sweaters for goalposts. Every few months, the academy would cut players they didn't think were good enough. It was nerve-wracking, and saying goodbye to friends was sad.

Marcus worked incredibly hard and stayed focused on his dream for many years. Then, one match day, when he was 18 years old, some of his teammates were injured. This meant that Marcus was called up to play for the first team. He made quite an impression, scoring two goals. Then, three days later, he played again and scored twice more. And the goals just kept on coming.

When he signed his new contract shortly after, his future at Manchester United was secured. With a huge salary, he finally had the money he needed to help his family.

In June 2020, Marcus was at home recovering from a back injury. It was during one of the Covid-19 lockdowns when everyone had to stay at home.

Marcus was watching Boris Johnson, the English Prime Minister, on TV. He said he was going to put a stop to free school meals. Marcus was stunned. He knew from experience that free school meals helped a lot of families who were struggling to buy food. No child should go hungry. He had to do something. He had to say something.

So, Marcus wrote to the Prime Minister, asking him to change his mind. He explained that it was important to protect people who find themselves in a situation where they cannot protect themselves. He explained that he had grown up in a challenging situation and had personal experience of soup kitchens and food banks.

He did not shout. He did not scream. He stood up for what was right and for what mattered, quietly and with dignity. And eventually, the government listened and overturned their decision.

Next, he turned his attention to books. When he was younger, his family didn't have the money to buy books. He did not read a book until he was 17 years old. Not one. But Marcus realized that books could have helped him. So, he decided to raise money to buy books for kids who do not have access to them. He hopes the children reading them will be inspired and realize that there is a world beyond their struggles.

Marcus, the softly spoken soccer player, has become a game-changer on and off the pitch. He speaks up in his quiet way for the people who do not have a voice. He has helped not just his mother have a better life but thousands and thousands of other people, too.

Greta Thunberg

(born 2003)

Greta felt like she was invisible. She spent a lot of time on her own and didn't have any friends. Greta hardly spoke at all. Her classmates at school in Stockholm, Sweden, thought she was nerdy and strange. Everyone just ignored her—it was as though Greta didn't exist.

When she was eight years old, Greta started watching nature documentaries. Seeing polar bears struggling to survive on the melting ice in the Arctic upset her. She felt distressed watching the fish in the ocean being poisoned by tiny pieces of plastic. Greta dug deep into her dismay, spending hours every day reading and researching.

Pictures of our planet in peril stuck in Greta's head. They were so firmly lodged that she couldn't feel happy anymore. She stopped playing the piano and was barely eating. All she could think about was the environment.

Greta lost a lot of weight and became very weak. Her parents were beside themselves with worry. They stayed home to look after her and encouraged her to eat. Sitting by her bedside, they persuaded Greta to talk to them. Gradually, she began talking about the environment and how worried she was. She pleaded with her parents to do something.

The family agreed to stop eating meat and turn the lights off when they didn't need them to save electricity. Greta convinced her mum to stop traveling by plane, even though she often needed to for her work as an opera singer.

Despite the inconvenience, her family could see that these changes made Greta feel better. Their actions, no matter how small, made Greta realize

she could make a difference. She had a purpose.

Next, Greta entered a writing competition, where she wrote about climate change and why we need to start doing something about it. After that, she workshopped ideas to grab people's attention so that they would take action, too. She wanted politicians to do something—to take the climate crisis seriously—rather than just talk about it. So, she decided to go on strike and stopped going to school.

Nobody understood what Greta was doing, and, at first, nobody wanted to join her. Greta was unbothered. She decided to do it anyway. Before she started her protest in earnest, Greta ensured she knew what she was talking about in case she was challenged. She researched all the facts so nobody could catch her out or make her look foolish.

And then, in August 2018, Greta sat down on the steps in front of the Swedish Parliament building. She sat there for hours, all alone, next to her handmade stack of leaflets and her sign saying "Skolstrejk för klimatet", which means "School strike for climate".

Every day for three weeks, Greta sat on the steps of the parliament building with her schoolbooks, protesting. Her father would pop by when he could, bringing her food so she wouldn't get too hungry.

And then a funny thing happened. Gradually, people started to pay attention to the little girl sitting all by herself on the steps. They came to join her and sit with her in solidarity.

Greta's protest grew and grew. It grew in Sweden, then Scandinavia, then Europe, and then across the world. Greta's solo protest evolved into the Fridays for Future movement, with over 100,000 schoolchildren going on strikes in more than 100 countries, demanding that politicians do something to stop climate change. The tiny teenager who wondered if she was invisible started a global movement.

Catapulted into the limelight, Greta was now giving speeches to politicians and world leaders. At first, she was shy about sharing her ideas. Being so young, she initially struggled to get people to listen, but she's become much better at social interaction—she's had lots of practice.

Driven by her passion for change, Greta gets straight to the point whenever she speaks on important topics. She isn't intimidated by power, and she's not afraid of upsetting or offending people. She simply says what needs to be said. She's found her voice—and it's powerful indeed. Perhaps if she had been like everyone else, she wouldn't have had the focus and determination to protest and stand up for her beliefs. And perhaps if she had been easily intimidated, she wouldn't have had the courage to give her famous "How dare you?" speech to world leaders at the 2019 United Nations Climate Action Summit. Nobody can ignore her now.

You see, it doesn't matter how small you are or how small you feel. We can all make a difference.

Abraham Lincoln
(1809 – 1865)

Abraham was overwhelmed. He'd been working all day on the family farm in Kentucky, USA. Since his little brother and beloved mother had died, his father needed him more than ever.

He slumped onto the front step of their tiny shack in the woods, wiped his dusty brow, and sighed. He didn't mean to seem ungrateful, but this wasn't the kind of life he had imagined for himself. He wanted more from his life than living in the middle of nowhere in the deep, dark woods, scraping a living, battling the weather, fighting floods, and struggling with sickness.

Going to school was a privilege he did not have, so he taught himself to read. If he was going to be trapped here in this tiny log cabin, then at least he could escape and explore the world in his head.

The more he read, the more he learned and the more he grew. Abraham got taller, his ears grew bigger, and his feet expanded to a massive size 14! By the time he was a young man, Abraham was a towering 6ft 4in.

Life in the little log cabin started to feel cramped, and Abraham finally felt ready to step out into the big wide world. With no money, no qualifications, no friends, and no idea what he would do to earn money, Abraham stumbled from job to job. He had never felt more alone.

He worked on a boat, as a blacksmith, a postman, a surveyor, and in a store. And then, one day, he witnessed a slave auction where Black people were being sold for money as if they were animals or property. Abraham was shocked by the cruelty and the inhumanity. It dawned on him that he was

here on earth to stand up for people who could not defend themselves. He decided that he would become a lawyer.

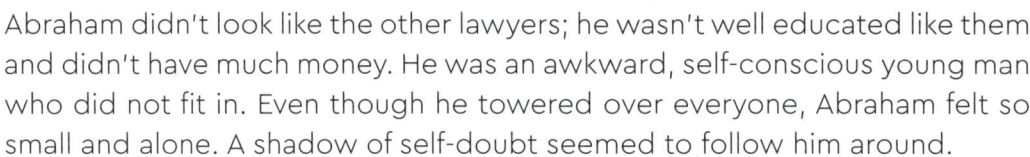

Unlike work on the farm, there was no dirt or digging involved in his work as a lawyer, but it was very tricky. Abraham didn't look like the other lawyers; he wasn't well educated like them and didn't have much money. He was an awkward, self-conscious young man who did not fit in. Even though he towered over everyone, Abraham felt so small and alone. A shadow of self-doubt seemed to follow him around.

Being a lawyer didn't involve sitting quietly and reading books. Abraham had to go out and find clients, speak confidently in court, and hopefully win some cases. In court, he would stumble over his words and jumble his arguments. Sometimes, no words would come out at all, and on occasion, Abraham would get so nervous that he'd have to race to the bathroom and vomit.

Abraham could not go back to the log cabin. So many people needed his help. So, he continued training and practicing, and gradually, over time, he got better at handling the pressure and his nerves. And he hardly ever lost his lunch!

Meanwhile, it was a bleak time in the USA. Black people were being sold as slaves and subjected to terrible cruelty. The American Civil War was raging, and people wanted to divide America into smaller chunks. Abraham had to do something. Being a lawyer was not enough. If he wanted to stop the war, keep America together, and put a stop to slavery, he would need to take another big step out of his comfort zone. If he wanted to make a real change, he would have to become a politician. No, scrap that. He was going to have to become the PRESIDENT!

It was a humongous challenge. On the one hand, public speaking helped Abraham to reach people and spread his message, but he hated the stammering, the shaking, and the sweating! He didn't love big events with lots of people, and he would often sit in silence in meetings and debates. One time, when he had to stand up to speak, he froze completely, blushed bright red, and just sat back down. Talk about being awkward!

But the American people needed him. In the face of slavery and war, his feeling shy didn't seem so significant. There were bigger issues at stake. And someone had to do something. It was time for Abraham to step up.

He planned his speeches meticulously. He made notes when he was out and about on little scraps of paper and popped them in his hat for safekeeping, and when he got home, he would glue them together. Abraham would practice his speeches out loud over and over until he knew them by heart.

He didn't shout or wave his arms about. He was calm and humble and became known as Honest Abe because he spoke the truth. People trusted him. Instead of trying to sound fancy, he explained himself logically and clearly. People liked him because they could understand what he was talking about. They could see that he sometimes got nervous, but they thought it made him more human and showed that he cared. The fact that he was quiet gave weight to his words. When he spoke, people listened.

Abraham persevered until he finally became a politician. Then, he persevered when he stood for president and lost. In 1860, he stood for president for the second time—and guess what? He won!

Abraham Lincoln became the sixteenth president of the United States of America. He grew into a great leader and a humble, kind, and honest man who eventually helped to abolish slavery and keep America together as one big country. And despite his nerves and awkwardness, he is remembered for giving some of the most moving, inspiring, and famous speeches of all time.

William Kamkwanba
(born 1987)

William lived in Masitala, a village in Malawi, Africa. There was barely any money, very little food, almost no water pumps, and no electricity. The lack of electricity meant there were no computers or televisions, and people had to use expensive batteries to power radios—and hair clippers.

The people in William's village felt helpless, worried, and hungry. Food was running out. William and his family had to survive on just one meal a day. Some families were dying from starvation.

To make matters worse, William had to deal with some of the bigger kids pushing him around. They called him names and teased him for being so quiet. If only he could find the strength to stand up to the bullies.

Inspiration struck. He asked one of the nicer kids to put a magic spell on him to give him powers. The boy performed the spell, but nothing magical happened when William confronted the bully. Instead, the bully punched William in the face. It seemed that if William wanted to brighten up his life, magic was not the answer. He would have to use his brain to find a solution.

People in the village always said that radios were powered by magic, but William was unsure. He decided to dismantle the family's radio to see how it worked. He peered inside, fiddled about with the electronics, took it to pieces, and put it back together again.

Word spread, and soon, people were asking William to fix their radios for them. William's mind was spinning. He wondered what else he could build or repair with just his hands and his brilliant mind.

> *"It turned out that William did not need magic. He had the power inside him all along. Like the wind, he just needed to find a way to harness it."*

Then, one night, William spotted someone riding a bicycle. There was a bright light shining on the handlebars. How was the light working? There was no way he would use a battery, as they were so expensive. When the man got off his bike and parked it, William snuck over to investigate.

He noticed an extra little wheel on the bike. It seemed that as the man pushed the pedals and the wheels turned, the extra little wheel turned too and generated electricity for the light.

The next day, William headed to the library to find out more. It turned out he had discovered something called a dynamo. William's brain started whirring, wondering if he could use a dynamo to generate electricity for a radio.

He set to work. He built a dynamo by linking a bicycle wheel to a radio. It worked! When the wheel turned, it made electricity and powered the radio. And it was free! All you needed were some legs to power it.

William continued his research. He started to think bigger. He wondered if he could somehow harness the wind and get it to turn a big wheel, like a dynamo, to create electricity. If it worked, his family could have a water pump to water the crops so they could grow more food. Perhaps a windmill could set the village free and save people's lives.

He had never seen a real-life windmill before, let alone built one, but William carried on regardless. He built a little model windmill to test his theory. Then, when that worked, he planned to build something much larger. With no money or spare parts, William headed to the scrapyard and searched the huge mountains of junk for pieces he could use.

Over time, he collected all the pieces he needed before he set to work building and welding the pieces together. The windmill was enormous! Next, he constructed a huge wooden tower and persuaded his friend Gilbert to help him lug the massive windmill to the top of the tower.

Everyone from the village crowded around, wondering what on earth was happening. Standing at the top of the tower, William spoke softly, telling the people below that he was going to generate electricity from the wind. Some could not hear him, others did not understand, and the rest thought he was talking nonsense.

But William did not care. He simply attached a lightbulb to the windmill. The magnificent blades began to turn, and the bulb lit up. William had done it! He had made electricity from the wind.

In that moment, everything changed. Now, people could power a water pump for the field. They could have clean water and better food. They would not go hungry anymore. They could even use mobile phones and computers —and get a decent haircut!

Word began to spread about William and his windmill. At first, he found all the attention uncomfortable. But he put his embarrassment to one side because he had more important things to think about. William spent his time showing people in lots of other villages how to build windmills so they could save their communities too.

It turned out that William did not need magic. He had the power inside him all along. Like the wind, he just needed to find a way to harness it.

TAKE A STAND

Quiet Reflection

Take a moment to think about what matters to you. How can you take a stand? Answer these questions to help you.

The problem in my community
that I want to solve is . . .

The changes I want to make
in the world around me are . . .

Thinking about this issue makes me feel . . .

I know I am lucky because . . .

The people I would like to help are . . .

I feel very strongly about . . .

I am going to speak up for . . .

I am going to help by . . .

In the next week, I will . . .

When I'm older, I want
to be known for . . .

DO IT YOUR WAY

Lewis Hamilton
(born 1985)

Racing superstar Lewis Hamilton grew up in a town called Stevenage, England. It was a predominantly white area, with very few Black people. At school, the other children were not always kind to him. They called him names and threw stuff at him. The bigger, stronger kids would push him around and pick on him. When it came to soccer, even though he was a good player, nobody would choose him for their team.

Lewis felt alone and confused, like he did not belong at his school or in his town. He did not tell anyone how he felt, not even his parents, because he doubted anyone would understand, and he didn't want them to think he was weak. So he hid his emotions and squashed them down inside, but they did not go away. They ballooned and got bigger while Lewis became quieter.

Lewis's parents were separated, but his dad, Anthony, would visit regularly. When he did, they bonded over their mutual love of cars—Anthony loved motor racing. When Lewis was five years old, his dad bought him a radio-controlled toy car. Not content to just race around the house or the street, Lewis entered races. He came second in the Radio-Controlled Car Championship, competing against grownups!

Anthony took Lewis go-karting so that he could drive a real car on his own for the first time. Lewis loved it! Seeing how happy it made Lewis encouraged his dad to buy him his very own go-kart, helmet, and racing suit. It was expensive but worth it.

Lewis finally had a way to channel his feelings. If the other kids tried to bump into him on the track or rough him up as they sped around, he tricked

them and zipped past. He could get around the track the quickest, and this made him feel formidable. When he was behind the wheel, Lewis felt unbeatable.

Lewis soon told his dad he wanted to be a professional racing driver. His dad believed in him and thought it was possible, so he made an agreement with his son. Anthony would do his utmost to support Lewis—he would juggle multiple jobs to earn enough for Lewis to race. He would take him to training and the races, and, in return, Lewis would work hard both on the track and at school.

One day, when he was ten years old, Lewis was invited to an awards ceremony in London to collect some trophies. Ron Dennis, the boss of the McLaren Mercedes Formula 1 team, was at the event, and Lewis plucked up the courage to speak to him. Lewis introduced himself, asked for his autograph, and told him that one day, he would like to race for his team. Mr Dennis signed his name in Lewis's book and left him a note to give him a call in nine years. However, only three years later, Lewis joined the McLaren program for young drivers!

Legendary Formula 1 team owner Eddie Jordan was worried that Lewis was not confident enough to be a champion. He said that a champion's self-belief should overtake everything. But Lewis was not arrogant. He was calm and quiet. And it turns out being quiet was perfectly fine.

When Lewis was 22 years old, he made his first appearance as a Formula 1 driver for McLaren and became the first ever Black Formula 1 driver. In his first

"Everyone deserves to feel like they belong, no matter where they live, who they are, or what they look like."

year, he made it to the podium twice. The following year, he won his first World Championship and became the youngest-ever champion in F1 history!

Today, Lewis lives a wealthy lifestyle, jetting all over the world, hanging out with celebrities, living in fancy homes, and wearing expensive clothes. But underneath, he is still the same quiet person who likes to spend time on his own or with his family. He is close to his brother, Nicolas, who has cerebral palsy—a condition that affects development, coordination, and movement. He goes to every race, and Lewis says that Nicolas is his biggest inspiration.

Lewis has come a long way since his karting days. So far, he has won seven World Drivers' Championships and holds the record for winning the most races, pole positions, and podium finishes. He is the most successful British driver in the history of Formula 1 racing!

Now that he has a social following and people respect him for his driving abilities, Lewis speaks out against racism, and people listen to him. He is also campaigning to encourage young Black people to get involved in motorsports. Everyone deserves to feel like they belong, no matter where they live, who they are, or what they look like.

Beatrix Potter

(1866–1943)

Children's author Beatrix Potter was supposed to grow up and become a respectable young lady. She was told that she ought to marry someone sensible, drink lots of tea, learn embroidery, and make small talk. She was supposed to lead a small, simple life.

As a child, Beatrix's thoughts and ideas were unimportant to her parents. They thought her role in life was to look pretty. They decided not to send her to school like her brother. Instead, she would stay at home and be taught all the skills she would need to become a housewife by her governess.

This plan struck Beatrix as incredibly dull and unfair. Rather than tell anyone about her feelings, Beatrix scribbled furiously in her journals. She wanted so much more from her life. Beatrix wanted to be independent and have a career, not be an accessory on a man's arm. She was not a bangle or a bracelet—she was a person!

At home, young Beatrix was left to her own devices. Spending so much time alone was not good for Beatrix. Her social skills shriveled up. Her shyness skyrocketed. With no real lessons or schoolwork—and no human friends— she spent her days isolated in her room, collecting and learning about animals. She studied them in detail, writing about them and creating intricate illustrations. Filled with snakes, hedgehogs, bats, frogs, bees, birds, and beetles, her room looked more like a zoo or a laboratory than a bedroom. These furry, scaly, and spiky little creatures became her best friends.

When her little brother, Bertram, went off to boarding school, Beatrix stole his microscope so that she could pore over plants, algae, mushrooms, beetles, bats, spiders, moths, and weasels. She observed tiny wings, bodies, and antennae, creating incredibly intricate and scientifically accurate paintings of what she saw.

Every summer, Beatrix's family would go to the Lake District in the north of England. Away from the city, Beatrix could run wild, ride ponies, and roam the countryside in search of new fluffy-tailed creatures to study.

The years passed, and then when Beatrix was 19 years old, she developed an inflammatory condition called rheumatic fever and was confined to her bed for weeks. Never had she felt so sad and alone. As Beatrix floated in and out of sleep, she had vivid dreams of the animals she had studied. She dreamed of an imaginary world of mischief and mayhem, with rebellious rabbits in jackets, tiny kittens in mittens, and dastardly foxes with fiendish schemes.

As she recovered, Beatrix put these imaginings to one side so that she could study mushrooms and toadstools. She had a theory that fungi grew in the same way as mold, and she wanted to present her ideas to the scientists at the Royal Botanic Gardens, Kew. Trying to ignore her shyness, she mustered up the courage to challenge their current theories, but unsurprisingly, the experts did not take this young girl seriously.

One day, Beatrix heard that the son of her old governess was unwell. Knowing what it was like to be bedridden, Beatrix decided to cheer him up by writing him a story about an unruly little rabbit called Peter.

The story was so good that they pleaded with Beatrix to write more. As she wrote and illustrated the tales of the mischievous

Peter Rabbit, Beatrix sensed that this was her opportunity to create a future for herself. This was her ticket to freedom!

Once her book was finished, Beatrix began her search for a publisher. The first company she approached was not interested. Nor were the next five. However, Beatrix did not give up. She was no longer the meek Beatrix trapped in her bedroom—she had gone rogue, like Peter Rabbit!

Beatrix came up with a plan to get her book in front of people without the help of a publisher. She had 250 copies printed and gave them out to store owners and people she thought might like them. Luckily, people loved her Peter Rabbit stories and wanted more.

Beatrix knew exactly what she wanted her books to look like. They needed to be small enough for children to hold and printed with full-color illustrations on the best quality paper. Eventually, she found a publisher who listened to her vision.

Once the contract was sorted, Beatrix wrote many more stories, including *The Tale of Squirrel Nutkin*, *The Tale of Benjamin Bunny,* and *The Tale of Mrs Tiggy-Winkle*. In total, she wrote and illustrated 28 stories. She is still one of the world's best-loved children's authors and has sold an incredible 250 million books!

Beatrix made a lot of money from the sale of her books—enough to move to the Lake District and buy her own house and land. In the countryside, she was completely independent and able to be herself. She could live her life exactly as she wanted, surrounded by the wildlife she loved.

Frédéric Chopin
(1810–1849)

The Chopin family lived happily on the grounds of the Saxon Palace in Warsaw, Poland. Unfortunately, their son Frédéric faced many health challenges. He often experienced sickness after eating certain foods and had frequent headaches and coughs.

Frédéric's parents tried to lift his spirits with music, with Mr Chopin playing the flute and violin and Mrs Chopin playing the piano. His mother taught him to play the piano when he was just four years old, and he took to it like a swan to water. By the time he was six years old, he was already writing and composing complex pieces of music.

Word soon spread about the young piano genius, and Frédéric was invited to give informal concerts at wealthy people's houses. Unfortunately, Frédéric did not like this. He would worry about his performances for days—and sometimes even weeks before. It seemed like he was destined to play the piano in private.

Despite his nervousness, Frédéric's fondness for the piano remained. In fact, tinkling the ivories made him feel joyful. He continued studying at a special music school, where his skills improved immensely.

Unsurprisingly, his piano playing was very delicate for such a sensitive boy. But, at a time when it was fashionable to bash on piano keys with passion, not everyone understood Frédéric's refined way of playing.

Once he graduated from college, Frédéric was ready to go out into the world and make a living as a professional pianist. He traveled around Warsaw,

Vienna, and Berlin before settling in Paris. He took his favorite piano with him on his travels to make him feel more comfortable away from home.

In those days, talented musicians made money giving concerts, but Frédéric shied away from big audiences. His health problems also meant that he did not have the energy for huge concert halls. In fact, he only gave about thirty big concerts in his whole life! Big concerts stressed him out, and he would spend ages worrying about what he was going to wear. On the rare occasion he gave a concert, he would invite his friends to perform so that he was not alone.

At first, Frédéric worried his success would be squashed because of his reluctance to take to the big stage, but his performance and compositions were better suited to playing in small, intimate venues. He preferred to play the piano at small gatherings, in the salons of wealthy Parisians, or in his apartment for people who appreciated his sensitivity and delicate style. To make himself feel more comfortable, he would insist that the room be softly lit with candles, and sometimes, he would even blow out the candles so that he could perform in the shadows.

Instead of fretting about fame, Frédéric chose to focus on composing beautiful music. After all, there was nothing more enjoyable than creating music, and it was something he could do by himself. He also began teaching music to people who could afford to pay him and discovered that he much preferred helping people than being in the spotlight himself. As a teacher, Frédéric was kind and encouraging—and expensive! He encouraged his students to play in a relaxed and refined way, like him.

"Frédéric created the music he needed, and now—because he was brave enough to share it with us—we can enjoy it too."

Frédéric also knew he was terrible at singing his own praises, so he asked his good friend Franchomme for help. Franchomme loved Frédérics music and was happy to put together a catalog of his amazing compositions to share his music. Frédéric did not brag about his talents—he preferred to let his music do the talking. But sometimes, even musical geniuses need a little marketing help!

In Paris, Frédéric was shy around people he did not know, but when he was hanging with his few close friends, he was relaxed and chatty, and he loved to gossip! Frédéric knew who he was, what he needed, and when to ask for help. He became close friends with fellow musician Franz Liszt, and they lived down the road from each other for many years. Socializing was not Frédéric's cup of tea, so if he was invited to a big party, he would drag Liszt along, too.

Frédéric knew that music could calm him down when he felt stressed, so he wrote music to help ease his own anxiety and worries. Today, experts believe that listening to Frédéric Chopin's music is good for our wellbeing and that it soothes us when we are stressed or afraid. Frédéric created the music he needed, and now—because he was brave enough to share it with us —we can enjoy it, too.

Naomi Osaka

(born 1997)

Leonard Francois had a plan for his daughters Naomi and Mari. They would become tennis champions like Venus and Serena Williams. To begin working toward this goal, he moved his family from Japan to America when Naomi was three years old. Just like Mr Williams, he began teaching his daughters to play tennis. He may not have been a professional coach, but he was certainly determined.

Naomi and Mari practiced for eight hours a day, hitting hundreds and hundreds of balls up and down the court. The girls stopped going to school and studied in the evening after they had finished their training.

When Naomi was on the tennis court, hitting the furry yellow ball back and forth, she was in her element. Playing tennis made her feel happy, relaxed, and powerful, and gradually, very gradually, all her hard work paid off. Naomi became so good at tennis that she skipped the junior competitions and went straight into the senior tournaments.

Unfortunately for Naomi, competitive tennis is a lot more complicated than just hitting a ball. Tournaments involve lots of pressure, traveling to new places, big crowds, and speaking to journalists. However, Naomi was a quiet, softly spoken person who struggled with public speaking. She also disliked noise—being loud was not her style.

Traveling to new places filled Naomi with uncertainty. Meeting new people was difficult. Stepping into the changing rooms at a tournament was scary because everything was so strange and new. Even working out where to sit or where to put her things made Naomi feel flustered.

Talking to journalists is part of being a professional tennis player—it is something you must do. However, when interviewers asked Naomi questions, her shyness would set in. She worried about what to say and whether her answers would be good enough. She would worry so much that the words would get caught in her mouth, and nothing would come out.

When Naomi won a competition, she had to give a speech to the crowd —sometimes to thousands of people! Naomi felt like the most awkward person in tennis. She would get the giggles and talk about random things that popped into her head, like computer games, or she would get fidgety and only be able to give one-word answers.

Naomi tried to manage her feelings of stress and being overwhelmed by wearing big headphones. She aimed to drown out the noise of the crowd by creating an imaginary bubble around herself so she could concentrate on playing tennis. For a while, it worked.

Naomi started to win big games and became famous for having an incredibly fast serve. She won awards and even went on to beat her hero, Serena Williams. Naomi became the number one female player in the world!

But the more matches she won, the more people expected of Naomi, and the more interviews and press conferences she had to do. It was horrible.

One day, during an important match at The French Open, Naomi was struggling to find her form. She kept making mistakes. Suddenly, someone in the crowd shouted at Naomi that she sucked. Naomi got very upset.

After the game, Naomi refused to attend the press conference. The tournament organizers were cross with Naomi, but she did not care. Something had to change, so she decided to withdraw from the competition and take a break from playing tennis.

Instead of hiding away at home, feeling embarrassed or ashamed, Naomi decided to be honest and write about her feelings. She explained that she found speaking to the press difficult and was struggling with social anxiety. Sports people rarely talk about their struggles, perhaps because they do not want people to think they are weak. But writing openly like this made Naomi feel strong.

Because of Naomi, others shared their struggles, too. Her actions helped people to realize that celebrities and athletes are real people with real emotions and feelings.

For the next few months, Naomi took time to relax and look after herself. She spent time with her friends and family baking bread, cooking, reading, meditating, drawing, and designing amazing clothes.

Naomi finally understood that her quiet voice had the power to help people who could not stand up for themselves, so she started speaking up about the issues that were important to her. And when she felt ready, Naomi started playing tennis again—this time for fun.

DO IT YOUR WAY

Quiet Reflection

It's now time to reflect on the previous chapter and finish these sentences to help you work out what you want to do and how you can achieve that your own unique way.

My ideal way to relax is . . .

My favorite way to socialize is . . .

My preferred way to spend my weekend is . . .

My favorite way to study is . . .

My ideal way to celebrate success is . . .

My perfect birthday celebration would be . . .

I feel happy when I am . . .

A situation I find tricky is . . .

DON'T GIVE UP

Kōhei Uchimura
(born 1989)

From the moment he could roll over, Kōhei started swinging from the bars of his little bed as if he were a gymnast. It was no surprise as gymnastics ran in his blood—both his parents and his older sister were gymnasts. Flinging himself through the air was his destiny.

Kōhei's parents ran a sports club for kids in the Nagasaki Prefecture of Japan, and when he was just three years old, they took him along. When it came to trampolining and bouncing about, he was very enthusiastic. His parents offered to take him swimming or to play baseball, but he refused. He just wanted to do gymnastics.

When he was not bouncing, swinging, or rolling, Kōhei was thinking about bouncing, swinging, and rolling. When he got home, he would watch gymnastics on TV, dreaming of becoming a professional gymnast and performing amazing moves.

He was a quiet boy who did not talk much or smile very often. He found it hard to talk to the other gymnasts because he was too shy. Instead, he would just keep quiet and focus on his training.

Kōhei felt comfortable when both his parents were at the gym, but if they were not there, he would get worried and agitated. Talking to the other coaches was difficult for him, so he used body language and hand signals to explain what he wanted to say.

Progress was slow. Routines that other kids would master in a few minutes would take Kōhei ages to figure out, and sometimes, he would forget his

> *"As he grew in confidence, Kōhei discovered that . . . his fears would disappear, and he could get on with doing what he does best."*

moves and start crying. When he entered his first competition, at the age of six, he came last. Sometimes, he felt like backflipping out of the door and never coming back. Occasionally, he would mess up or fall off the apparatus and hurt himself. Or he would have negative thoughts and wonder if he could do it at all. But he never gave up.

Kōhei realized that talent is nothing without hard work, so he studied and worked harder than anyone else, figuring things out at his own pace. He used a teddy bear to replicate complex moves, bending and positioning the bear into different poses and then drawing them in his notebook. He studied hours and hours of videos of the Olympic gold medalist Naoya Tsukahara's routines. He practiced endlessly on the trampoline at home, and eventually, things started to fall into place. Kōhei had found his gymnastics groove.

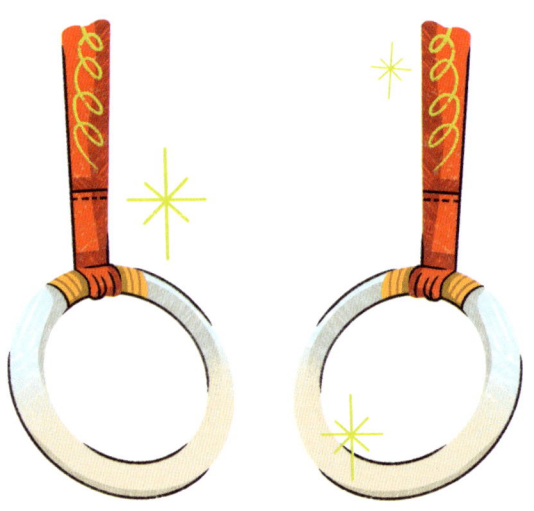

However, there was an obstacle in his way, and it was not the vault or the pommel horse. Kōhei did not like performing in front of people other than his mother. How would he cope at a competition when even the word itself made him feel sick?

He needed to work on his mindset as if it were a muscle, so he changed the way he viewed competitions. He reframed them to be his chance to show people how hard he had been working.

He started to view nerves differently. When he was nervous, he felt the same feelings as when he was excited. He decided to see his pounding heart and fidgety feet as a sign that he was delighted to be there, doing what he loved.

Kōhei found that listening to music and doing some quiet visualizations helped him relax, and he realized that being part of a team made him feel more confident and comfortable.

As he grew in confidence, Kōhei discovered that once he was out there on the apparatus, his fears would disappear, and he could get on with doing what he does best. When he performed his routine, he felt composed. All thoughts of medals, judges, and people watching would disappear. Instead, his mind was focused on his gymnastic moves and on producing a perfect performance.

When he was 18 years old, Kōhei qualified to represent Japan at the Olympics, where he won a silver medal. By the time he retired, he had won seven Olympic medals and 21 World Championship medals. He was so good that people called him Superman, and he is now famous all over the world for being one of the greatest gymnasts of all time.

Even though he is famous, Kōhei's biggest fan will always be his mother. Whenever she watched her son perform, she would get over-excited and jump about, noisily waving banners and flags. She even fainted when he won a gold medal! Kōhei was a little embarrassed, but even the greatest gymnast in the world needs his mother.

Taylor Swift
(Born 1989)

Once upon a time, in a big house on a Christmas tree farm in Pennsylvania, USA, there lived a kind-hearted girl with long, blonde hair. She was destined to become one of the world's most influential singer songwriters.

The little girl was called Taylor. She spent her days riding horses, running free outside, singing, and dancing. She also dreamed up stories and spent hours alone in her bedroom, snuggling under her patchwork quilt and making up fairy tales. You couldn't imagine a happier, more idyllic childhood.

Music was woven through the fabric of Taylor's life. Her grandma was an opera singer, and Taylor loved going to church to listen to her perform. Taylor dreamed that one day she would become a singer, too.

Then, when she was six years old, Taylor discovered a song called "Blue" by a young country singer named LeAnn Rimes. Taylor's life was changed forever. She became obsessed with country music, listening to female country artists like Shania Twain and Faith Hill. These singers told powerful stories through their song lyrics.

Taylor started going to singing and acting classes, entering singing competitions, and taking part in musical theater shows. She especially loved doing karaoke in front of an audience. Determined to be famous, she entered the singing competition at a local country inn every week for a year and a half until she eventually won.

Taylor was unstoppable when she was singing, but she struggled at school. Although she was a friendly person, people were mean to her. They said she was weird and did not understand why she liked country music. People would avoid her, ignore her, and even hide from her. They called her horrid names, said she had frizzy hair, threw stuff at her in the corridor, and pushed her around. As a result, Taylor spent lots of time alone and even ate lunch in the school restroom.

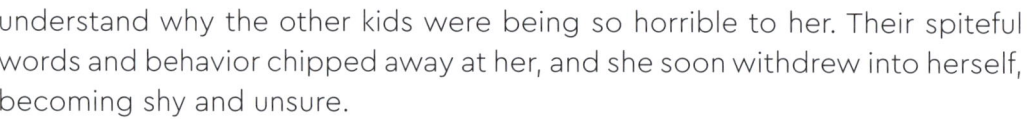

Understandably, Taylor was sad a lot of the time, and her confidence was affected. She didn't understand why the other kids were being so horrible to her. Their spiteful words and behavior chipped away at her, and she soon withdrew into herself, becoming shy and unsure.

Taylor didn't know what to do with all the horrible feelings swirling around inside her. But then, one day, she picked up a pen and started scribbling everything down. She wrote about being left out and picked on, having no friends, and feeling like she wasn't good enough. Taylor filled notebook after notebook—all her sadness and rage poured onto the page.

When Taylor was eleven years old, her mother took her to Nashville, Tennessee, the home of country music. They rented a car and drove to all the record companies. Taylor was determined to make her dreams come true despite how her bullies made her feel. She walked up to the receptionists, put on a brave face and said, "Hey, I'm eleven, and I want a record deal. Call me."

Taylor's plan didn't work, but being told no only made her more determined. All she had to do was figure out how to stand out. It was then that Taylor realized that no country music singers were singing about what it was like to be young. If she played guitar and sang songs about her experiences, maybe people would listen.

Taylor had no idea how to play a guitar, but that didn't stop her. She persuaded someone who came to her home to fix the family computer to teach her. He showed her three basic chords—and she was off! Taylor fell in love with the guitar. It turned her poems and stories into songs. She practiced and practiced for hours at a time.

Taylor's parents supported her dream of becoming a country singer, so they moved to be closer to Nashville. With iconic music venues and record labels nearby, Taylor was inching closer to her dream. She started going to a different school and made some new friends, including her new best friend, Abigail. Unfortunately, there were lots of bullies in her new school, too.

But this time, when the bullies struck, Taylor knew what to do. She took her bad experiences and turned them into songs. Writing helped Taylor feel better. Music gave her power over the people who were mean to her and helped her overcome her shyness.

And then, when Taylor was just 14 years old, something amazing happened. She was singing at the famous Bluebird Café in Nashville when a record producer heard her perform. He was so impressed that he offered her a record deal!

Her first single was released in June 2006 and her first album came out later that year. It reached number five in the bestseller charts! Since then, Taylor has released album after album and has gone on to sell millions of records.

Even though Taylor is one of the most famous people on the planet, she loves nothing more than spending time with her family, best friend, and fluffy cats (who she carries around in her backpack). Her songs are made up of all her experiences, good and bad. She shows us that nobody's life is perfect, and things don't always go according to plan. But when things go wrong, we don't give up. We dust ourselves down, shake it off, and keep trying.

James Dyson
(born 1947)

When James Dyson was nine years old, his father became extremely unwell and took the train to London to go to the hospital, where he soon died.

Poor James was struck with grief and was terribly afraid. Without his father, what would become of his family? His mother had no money and three children to look after. They grew their own vegetables and kept chickens so they could eat eggs, but there was no TV, fancy toys, or shiny new things. The house was often cold because heating it was too expensive, and they didn't have a refrigerator to keep food fresh.

James' father had been a teacher at a boarding school where James studied. When his father died, he was allowed to stay on for free, even though his mother did not have the money to pay for tuition. James worked hard at school, but he worried that he was not good enough and that he did not deserve to be there. His fear of making mistakes and being judged made it hard for him to speak in class and share his ideas.

When he was not studying, James loved to go running along the coastline. Running made him feel strong and free, helping him forget his worries and anxieties. He kept going even when he was tired and in pain from a fall. Running taught him determination and that giving up was not an option.

During the school break, James would spend hours playing with his dad's old tools. He made model gliders and planes with real engines. He loved figuring out how things worked, dismantling them, rebuilding them, and coming up with new ideas. With nobody to show him what to do, he messed around and experimented just for fun. There, in the shed,

he realized that making mistakes was OK because that is how you learn and improve.

Over the years, James created all kinds of things. When he was a grown up, he was in the garden with his wife one day, and his wheelbarrow kept getting stuck in the mud. It was exasperating! He removed the wheel and replaced it with a big plastic ball. Just like that, he had invented a brand-new kind of wheelbarrow, with a wheel that would not get clogged up with mud or go rusty. He called it the Ballbarrow.

James was on a roll! Everywhere he looked, he saw problems to solve.

The fancy new vacuum cleaner that he had bought was no good. It kept getting blocked because of the bag inside, and then it would not suck dirt up anymore. He was determined to fix it, but how?

For weeks, he could not stop thinking about it, and then inspiration struck when he was in a sawmill, waiting to have some wood chopped. James noticed that to stop the air from getting filled with sawdust, the wood-choppers had installed massive cyclone fans to clean the air. James started to wonder if something smaller but similar could work inside a vacuum cleaner.

He dashed home and tried to make something out of cardboard, which he attached to his vacuum. It made a small difference, but this was just the beginning. He tweaked his design and made another prototype that worked a little bit better. And another. And another. All that running meant that James never gave up. He kept trying and learning from his mistakes. He did not care if people thought he was weird—he was determined.

5,127 (yes, you read that right) prototypes, and 15 years later, James had invented the first bagless vacuum cleaner. It looked awesome—you could see all the dust inside. James had finally done it! Talk about commitment.

Now, he just had to sell it to some big companies. He would have to stand up in front of them, tell them about his idea, and ask them to give him some money. It was scary because James got nervous when speaking in public. Instead of trying to give a talk, he simply showed them a model.

Sadly, this approach did not work. The companies told James they were not interested and they preferred their existing designs. They said people would not want to see all the dust and dirt from their carpets inside the machine.

But this wasn't the whole truth. Secretly, they were interested, but they did not want to pay for his idea. Instead, they set to work copying his designs.

When James found out that Hoover had copied his idea, he was cross. Scrap that—he was livid! It had taken him many years and so much hard work to create his vacuum cleaner, so it did not seem fair. It was then that he discovered a mightiness within that he did not know he had.

He took Hoover to court even though he knew it would be difficult because he was just one person and Hoover was a massive company. But he knew that he had to stand up for himself even if he was scared and worried.

And guess what—he won! Hoover had to pay him millions of pounds and stop making their rip-off product. Ha!

Since then, James has sold millions of Dyson vacuum cleaners worldwide. He has won lots of awards and made an enormous amount of money. James hasn't stopped there—he has continued solving problems with other inventions, including fans, washing machines, and blow dryers. All his products look cool, but the most important thing about them is that they work extremely well. James is proof that, if at first you do not succeed, try, try, and try again. Never give up, and do not let the big guys push you around.

Savannah Marshall

(born 1991)

Creeping tentatively up the steps to her local boxing gym, Savannah could hear the pounding of loud music and the sounds of pads, bags, and people being punched. Thwack! Kapow! Oof!

She put one foot in front of the other and took one step at a time. Savannah was not someone who took risks or even spoke to people she did not know. Each little step forward felt like a giant leap into the unknown.

Savannah's shyness had her in a headlock. She was so shy that if a teacher even mentioned her name at school, she would blush the color of a beetroot. Although she was tall and sporty, Savannah battled with the social side of things. She struggled to talk to the other kids, the teachers, and even her football and netball teammates.

But, on that day in Hartlepool—a seaside town in the Northeast of England—Savannah realized she was stronger than she thought. She tiptoed inside, found the coach, and asked to join in. The conversation did not go as planned—he told her that girls did not belong there and yelled at her to leave.

Savannah may have been shy, but she was not afraid of people shouting. You see, Savannah's large family was noisy. They taught her that anything worth having is worth fighting for. Savannah was set on proving that she was capable, so without saying a word, she put on some boxing gloves and just started training.

Every day, Savannah rode across town on her bike to the boxing gym. No matter what the weather, she would make the journey. There was no

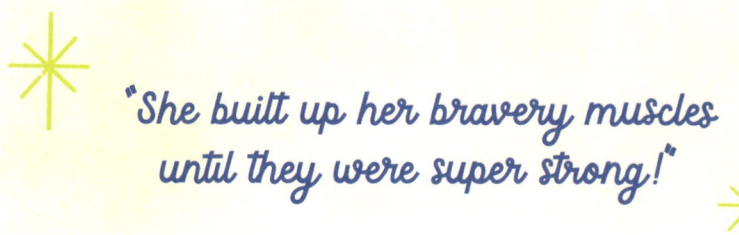

"She built up her bravery muscles until they were super strong!"

girls' changing room, so she decided she would rather stay stinky until she got home. Eventually, she was fit enough to run all the way to the gym, train, and run all the way back! She trained harder than anyone else—skipping, running, punching, and lifting. Savannah had convinced everyone that she deserved to be there.

All that grueling hard work paid off, and Savannah became invincible in the boxing ring. Nobody could beat her. Her crushing power and devastating punches were infamous. People called her the Silent Assassin. She even had it written on her shorts.

Outside the ring, it was a different story altogether. Savannah was a bundle of nerves, anxiety, and self-consciousness. The thought of people watching her made Savannah wobble, and before her fights, she would vomit. What if she messed up? What if she made a fool of herself? What if she let everyone down? She avoided telling anyone about her competitions. Her coach had to call her parents in secret so they could come and watch without Savannah knowing.

All those worries were a big distraction. If her opponents sensed weakness, they could use it to their advantage. Savannah's coach taught her to focus like a laser on the job in front of her. If she was strong enough to fight, she was strong enough to forget about her fears and worries. She blocked the audience and their possible opinions out of her mind, and it worked. Savannah started to worry less and have more fun.

Soon, Savannah was competing all over the world. In 2012, she won the gold medal at the World Championships in China. But traveling was troublesome because Savannah hated being away from home and longed to be back with her family.

At the 2012 London Olympics, she was away from her family once more, and homesickness set in. In the ring, instead of focusing on her fighting, she started thinking about the audience and the fact that thousands and thousands of people were expecting her to win the gold medal. It all went wrong. She was knocked down, and she lost. All Savannah wanted to do was go home to her family and climb into bed.

After that setback, Savannah was incredibly disappointed, but she did not give up. She kept training in the gym and practiced traveling, fighting in front of big crowds, and giving interviews. She even went to live and train in Las Vegas, USA, for six months. She built up her bravery muscles until they were super strong!

Now, Savannah is a professional boxer who loves to glare at her opponents and join in with trash talk during press conferences. She does not blush or back down.

Savannah became an undisputed champion and has won more belts than she could carry. In her spare time, she shares her experiences to encourage children who feel shy to build their social skills, confidence, and self-belief.

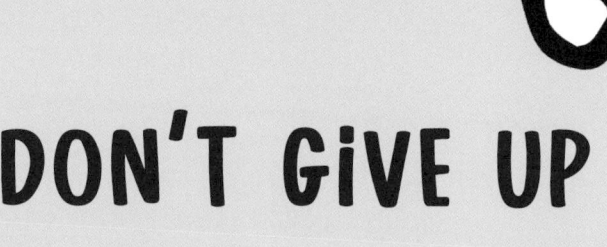

DON'T GIVE UP

Quiet Reflection

It's hard to push past tough times, pick yourself up and keep going. Take a moment to reflect on the previous chapter and finish these sentences to work out how you can keep going when things in your life get tough!

I felt like giving up when . . .

Some difficult situations I have faced include . . .

The last time I faced a setback, I learned . . .

When things feel difficult, I will focus on these positives . . .

In the past, I tried to fix a problem by . . .

It's important to keep trying because . . .

One time I did not give up was when . . .

Through determination I have become good at . . .

I am inspired by the resilience of [insert name] because they . . .

From now on, when I make a mistake, I will pick myself up and tell myself . . .

GLOW QUIETLY & BRIGHTLY

Mohandas "Mahatma" Gandhi

(1869–1948)

Mohandas lived in Porbandar, India. He feared lots of things, including snakes, robbers, teachers, and other children. He always slept with the lights on just in case something was lurking in the dark. Mohandas was also afraid of people laughing at him and of speaking in front of the class. At the end of each school day, he did not stick around to chat with the other children. As soon as the bell rang, Mohandas would grab his things and race back home to read his books.

One day, the inspector popped by his school for a surprise visit. Under pressure, the teacher asked the children to spell some difficult words, but Mohandas got stuck. Spotting this, his teacher whispered to one of the other children to sneak him the answer. But Mohandas did not want to cheat. Once the inspector left, the teacher was furious, but Mohandas did not care because he knew he had done the right thing. When it came to truth and justice, Mohandas was made of tough stuff.

When he was 18 years old, Mohandas's dad saw something special in his son and decided he should study in London, England, to become a lawyer. He thought Mohandas would make a great lawyer. But, if Mohandas felt like an outsider in India, it reached a whole new level when he arrived in London. Determined to fit in with the other students, he took speech lessons to change his accent, learned to dance, and bought lots of trendy clothes, including some shiny shoes, a flashy top hat, and a silver cane that he liked to twirl. So fancy!

He tried his best to be a good lawyer, but he was a bundle of nerves. Whenever Mohandas tried speaking to strangers, he fell silent. The first time he was in a courtroom, he got so stressed that he forgot what to say. When he tried to cross-examine the witness, he panicked and ran away. He had to give the client their money back.

It would have been easy for Mohandas to give up and go back home with his tail between his legs. But he did not. Instead, he headed to South Africa, where he was offered a new job.

On his way to the office, as he was sitting on the train holding his first-class ticket, the guard spotted him and kicked him off the train for being Indian. At that time, Indian people were treated terribly in South Africa by the white British and Boer people. They were beaten up, banned from traveling on the same trains, barred from voting, and forced to pay higher prices for things.

Mohandas was horrified. How could people be so cruel? At first, he was angry, but deep down, he knew anger was a waste of time. He had to do something. It was not in his nature to shout or be violent, so how could he help when he was just one small, shy person?

All he could do was be himself. So, he came up with a new way of standing up for what was right. He called it "passive resistance"—a way of fighting back without hurting anyone.

At first, he found making big speeches scary, so he wrote leaflets and letters instead. Then, when he felt more comfortable, he started speaking to a handful of people at a time. When fans praised him, he would feel super awkward and instead shift the focus onto those he was trying to help.

Fighting for what was right made him strong. He realized that it did not matter that he was afraid or nervous because he was battling for something important: truth and justice. He was standing up for people who needed him to be their voice because they did not have one. His purpose was more important than his fears.

Mohandas dedicated his whole life to making things better for the Indian population. He was determined to show those in charge when they were behaving in a horrible way and mistreating others. He defended the rights of his fellow citizens in South Africa and India against the British government.

Mohandas refused to see his shyness as a flaw. Instead, he decided to see it as his shield. He came to realize that being able to say what you mean in a few important words is a good thing—a message is clearer when there is no fluff. His shyness allowed him to be patient, to listen, and to think carefully about what he said.

Dressed only in a loin cloth and simple round glasses, he led marches of thousands and thousands of people. Gradually, he got used to being seen as a leader, and he would give speeches to massive crowds, stretching as far as the eye could see.

Mohandas became known for never shouting or screaming and never being aggressive or violent. In his quiet but extremely powerful way, he helped the people of India to become independent from Britain, even going to prison many times for speaking out against injustice. He was one of the most important leaders the world has ever seen.

People called him Mahatma, which means "great soul". He is proof that you do not need to shout to be heard. You do not need to be loud to make a difference. When he accepted who he was, he found his voice and unlocked the greatness within himself.

Ed Sheeran

(born 1991)

Growing up, Ed felt different from other kids—he had been born with a birthmark on his face, which made him stand out. As a child, he had an operation to remove it, but it went wrong, and they forgot to give Ed any anesthetic. This meant he could feel everything as they burned it off. Ouch!

The operation affected the development of one of Ed's eyes, and afterwards, he had to wear big, thick glasses. He was so traumatized by the operation that he developed a stutter. He knew what he wanted to say, but he couldn't get the words to flow—they got stuck.

At school, the teacher would ask the class something, and Ed would think, "Ooh, I know this!" He would put his hand up to answer, but when the teacher called on him, the words would get stuck again.

Some of the kids laughed at Ed. They chuckled at his stutter and teased him about his red hair, his giant glasses, and the fact that he was terrible at sports. Ed did not look or sound like the other kids. He cried at school every day.

When Ed's mother and father moved him and his big brother to a small town in Suffolk, England, they sent him to speech therapy to help with his stutter. They did not want him to change who he was, but they wanted to help him find his voice. Still, he struggled.

Then, when he was nine years old, Ed's uncle bought him The Marshall Mathers LP album by Eminem. Somehow, even though it is full of words that are inappropriate for a child, his uncle persuaded Ed's father to let him listen to it. They were amazed at how fast Eminem could rap!

Ed became obsessed with that album. He learned all the words off by heart—including the ones with bad words—and would sing them over and over. Something about the flow of the music, the rhythm, and the speed of the songs meant he did not stutter when he was singing.

Gradually, over time, he found that the more he practiced and drilled, he did not stutter when he was talking either. It is almost as if the music helped to re-wire his brain.

Ed became mesmerized by music. First, he learned to play the cello. Then, after seeing the legendary guitarist Eric Clapton on TV playing his song "Layla", he learned to play the guitar. He spent every spare minute of every day in his bedroom practicing, writing songs, and singing.

At first, Ed stayed in his bedroom, where he was safe and nobody could judge him. But he soon realized that if he wanted to be a famous musician, he needed people to listen to his music. Finally, Ed could see the benefits of looking different. If you want to be discovered, you need to be memorable. With his speedy lyrics and messy ginger hair, he was instantly recognizable.

Gradually, Ed's confidence skyrocketed. He joined a band, and the more skilled he became, the better he felt. Ed's dreams of becoming a professional musician were taking shape.

So, when he was fourteen years old, Ed stuffed a few clothes into a bag, slung his guitar over his shoulder, and set off all on his own on a musical mission to London. He knew that London was where he needed to be.

Whenever he could, Ed would play his music. He would play even the tiniest gigs and busk and sing all over town. But it was hard work. He did not have

"He is not flashy or flamboyant, he does not worry about the way he looks or sounds, he is just himself."

any money and would often end up sleeping rough in parks or on people's couches. Of course, he was determined, but there were many times he was tempted to give up and go back home to his parents.

Then, he had his aha moment! In 2010, Ed had a bright idea. He realized that social media was the key to growing his audience. He started posting videos online, and suddenly, the boy with red hair and a unique style started getting noticed by influential people and celebrities, too.

Ed had already been brave, but now it was time to take it to the next level. He decided he had to head to the USA. With no place to stay, no friends, and no record contract, he simply saved up his pennies from busking and booked a flight to Los Angeles.

Over in the USA, he continued plugging away at his music, playing gigs, and sending out demos, until an opportunity landed in his lap one day. Jamie Foxx, the famous actor and musician, heard his music and was fascinated. He invited Ed to use his studio so he could record an album and told all his famous friends about the scruffy British kid with the stunning songs.

All his hard work and bravery paid off. Ed's album became a huge hit. Since then, Ed has sold over 150 million albums and won stacks of awards. When he is on stage, singing to thousands of people, he has a way of bringing people together with his music. He is not flashy or flamboyant. He does not worry about the way he looks or sounds. He is just himself.

James Cleveland "Jesse" Owens

(1913–1980)

J.C. lived with his parents and his nine siblings in a tiny house on a farm in Alabama, USA. They lived squashed up together with not much room to move and not enough beds to go around.

J.C. was not a strong kid. He often struggled with breathing problems and pneumonia (inflammation of the lungs), and when he was five years old, he found a big lump on his chest. He ignored it for a few days, but it did not go away. Eventually, he told his mother that it was making it hard to breathe.

There were no doctors, and there was no hospital—even if there had been, his family would not have been able to afford to pay the fees. So, even though she was scared, J.C.'s mother took his health into her own hands and cut the lump out herself. The whole family prayed, and finally, the bleeding stopped.

Gradually, J.C. started to feel better and grew bigger and stronger. Everyone had to work on the farm so they could buy food, so by the time he was seven years old, J.C. was picking hundreds of pounds of cotton every single day.

When he was not working, he would race across the fields. It made him feel free. Nothing could stop him, squash him, or keep him small.

J.C's mother encouraged her husband to consider moving the family to Cleveland, Ohio, so they could have a better life. At long last, the family could afford a bigger house and eat properly. They were on the up!

In Cleveland, J.C. could go to school! Sure, he was the only ten year old in the class of much younger children—and he had to go to work after class—but J.C. was delighted to finally learn to read and write.

On the first day, the teacher asked what his name was. "J.C.", he replied softly. Misunderstanding his southern accent, she thought he said "Jesse" and J.C. was too shy to correct her. She was the teacher, after all, and he was the new kid. So, he let it slide and was called Jesse for the rest of his life.

One lunchtime, Mr Riley—the gym teacher—saw Jesse dashing around with his friends. He could not believe how fast he was! He invited Jesse to join the track team, but Jesse explained he had to work after school.

Mr Riley stood firm. He saw something special in Jesse, so he persuaded Jesse to train early in the morning before school. He thought the way Jesse ran was beautiful. It was as if he was flying! Mr Riley told Jesse to imagine the ground was on fire so that he would be light on his toes. He encouraged him to pretend to be like a racehorse with blinkers on, paying no attention to the competition, just running and running.

College scouts scrambled to sign Jesse. Nobody in Jesse's family had ever been to college before, but running gave him choices and opportunities beyond his wildest dreams. He later joined Ohio State University and was part of the track and field team.

Being a Black student at university was extremely challenging for Jesse due to racial prejudice—he was not permitted to live with white students. He was not allowed on the bus, in restaurants, or even in the same bathroom as white people, either.

But despite this cruelty, Jesse's talent was undeniable. He was soon appointed captain of the athletics team—the first Black person to hold this title. In his first year, he breezed through 42 races and won every single one! In total, he won eight National Championships during his time at university.

Then, in 1935, he did something incredible. Even though he was in a lot of pain from falling down the stairs and hurting his back a few days earlier, he broke three world records and equaled another in just 45 minutes. Now, that was a good day on the track. When he got home, he was in so much agony that he had to be carried up the stairs to bed.

Nobody was surprised when Jesse was selected to compete in the Berlin Olympics in August 1936. Nothing could stop him now—not even Adolf Hitler, the horrific dictator of Germany.

Hitler was a racist who believed that Jewish people, Black people, gay people, travelers, and disabled people shouldn't be allowed to live. He wanted to show that Germans, particularly those with white skin, blond hair, and blue eyes, were the best and that they would win all the medals.

Some people thought that the USA should not attend the Olympics that year because of Hitler, but Jesse wanted to go to prove that Black people were capable of greatness.

In the stadium, Jesse stood at the start line in front of Hitler and thousands of people waving Nazi flags, knowing that they hated him because of the color of his skin. He was so nervous. This was the most important day of his life. It was his chance to stand up to the cruel bullies—to have a voice.

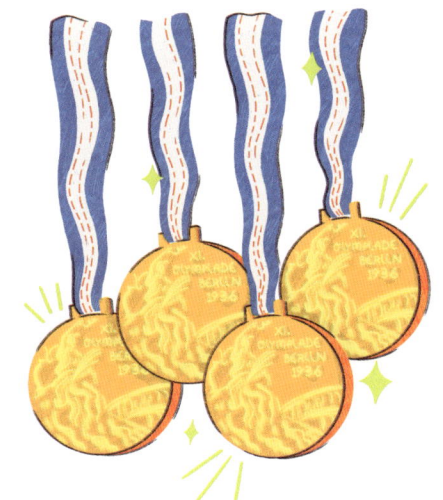

That day, he won gold medals for the 100-yard dash, the 200-yard dash, the long jump, and the men's relay. In total, he won four gold medals. Jesse Owens was the world's fastest person, much to Hitler's anger. Sometimes, actions really do speak louder than words.

Matthew Henson

(1866–1955)

Matthew was born to freeborn Black sharecroppers—formerly enslaved people working on another person's land and trading their crops for a place to live. Tragically, his mother died when he was four years old, and his father died a few years later. He had no family or friends, so at just 12 years old, Matthew left his home in Washington, DC, USA, in search of a brighter future.

Feeling scared and rather shy, with butterflies fluttering in his tummy, Matthew's hunger for adventure was bigger and stronger than his fears. He made his way to the docks and found a job working as a cabin boy on a ship that was heading for China. Feeling sorry for this quiet little kid, the captain took him under his wing. He taught Matthew how to read and write, and how to navigate, too. For the next few years, Matthew traveled all over the world, exploring the seven seas and learning all kinds of useful skills.

When the captain died, Matthew decided it was time to move on. He left the ship and went to work back on land in a fur store in Washington. Matthew was happy to have a sensible job that paid the bills, but he missed his old life at sea and yearned for adventure.

His life was changed forever when the famous explorer, Robert Edwin Peary, came into the store to purchase some furs. Peary was impressed by how calm, skilled, and intelligent Matthew was and offered him a job on his next expedition. First, they went to Nicaragua, South America, on a mapping mission, and then they trekked to Australia to track down some meteorites.

In those days, nobody knew what was at the North Pole. It was a complete mystery. Peary wanted to map the area and be the first person to set foot there. He was driven by fame and fortune, but Matthew was not. He was quietly curious about the world and loved learning new things.

Over the next 20 years, Peary and Matthew traveled to the Arctic across Greenland toward the North Pole 12 times. On each expedition, they dared to venture out a little bit further.

Matthew worked very hard, and on every trip, he tried his best to keep his team safe. He learned to hunt, cook, and mend clothes, as well as to look after a team of dogs and drive them in a sled. He knew the ice could easily damage the sleds, so he learned how to fix them and build them out of scrap material. He got used to working in the grimmest, harshest of ice storms.

Even so, there were incidents and accidents. Once, six of their teammates died. On another trip, they all nearly starved to death and ended up having to eat their dogs. Then, Peary got frostbite, and eight of his toes fell off. This Arctic exploration business was grueling and treacherous.

When he was not battling to survive, Matthew enjoyed the quiet times, observing and getting to know the customs of the Indigenous people who lived in Greenland. Unlike Peary, Matthew liked and respected them. He wrote about them in his notebook and even learned to speak their language. He wore their clothes, ate their food, and learned how to survive the harsh climate from them. They became his friends and called him Mahri-Pahluk, meaning "The Kind One".

In July 1908, a hobbling Peary and his quiet, brave, and dependable companion set off on their ultimate expedition to reach the North Pole. Matthew oversaw training people, building and maintaining the sleds, as well as hunting seals for people to eat, skinning the animals so they had furs to wear, fixing things, and communicating with the Indigenous team members.

Conditions were brutal, with temperatures reaching as low as −85°F. For six long, painful weeks, they trekked for 13 hours a day. They slept in igloos, but to stop frostbite from setting in, they had to wake themselves up all through the night to wiggle their fingers and toes.

Most of the team gave up and went home until only Peary, Matthew, and four guides remained. The howling wind whipped up rocks and flung them through the air, nearly knocking their heads off. The ice was hazardous, and it would often crack. Suddenly, areas of open water would appear, and the team would have to try to get across. Once, Matthew fell and plunged into the icy water. The guides saved him and helped him to quickly get dry before he turned into a giant human icicle.

At long last, on 6 April 1909, Matthew and Peary reached their goal: the North Pole. Matthew and the guides arrived first, with Peary trailing behind them —but in his eyes, Matthew was nothing but his assistant.

To make matters worse, on their return from their epic expedition, fame-hungry Peary told everyone he alone had conquered the North Pole. He ditched Matthew, stole all his photos, and banned him from giving interviews or writing about the trip. He silenced him, lapping up the praise, prizes, and glory. Meanwhile, the true hero, Matthew, was ignored.

Many years later, the truth finally came to light, and Matthew was presented with a medal by the US Navy and invited to the White House to meet the President. He even had a crater on the Moon named after him in honor of his contribution to science and exploration. Matthew, the quiet, conquering hero, finally got the recognition he deserved.

GLOW QUiETLY & BRiGHTLY

Quiet Reflection

Shy people can shine just as bright as confident people. Finish these sentences to remind yourself of times when you were able to glow quietly and brightly. Hopefully this will give you the confidence to continue shining brightly.

I was calm under pressure when . . .

I came up with a good idea when . . .

I listened well when . . .

I solved a tricky problem when . . .

People listened to me when I . . .

I was a loyal friend when . . .

I cared about other people when . . .

I prepared well when . . .

I helped others when . . .

I was creative when . . .

FINAL THOUGHTS

That's it! You made it!

Now that you've read about 40 softly spoken superheroes, you're officially ready to start your own Quiet Riot. Take the time to reflect on everything you have read and think about the things that make you unique and that inspire you. How can you make a difference just by being yourself?

Never forget that there is mightiness inside you. No more holding yourself back, keeping yourself small, or hiding away. No more wishing you were different or pretending to be something you're not.

It's time to follow your big, beautiful dreams. Say what's on your mind. Be strong and stand up for your beliefs. Be a little bit braver every day. Embrace your quiet power. Glow quietly but brightly. Change the world in your own quiet way.

And remember, you're not alone. Head over to shyandmighty.com and let me know how you are getting on. Who knows, maybe one day I'll be writing about your story!

Yours quietly,

Nadia x

About the Author

Nadia Finer knows what it's like to struggle with shyness, but instead of hiding away at home watching TV with her fuzzy dog, Bobby, she's embarking on a softly-spoken mission to help shy people be more mighty. Nadia has done some pretty cool stuff in her own quiet way—she has appeared on TV and radio, given talks in front of hundreds of people, and, in her spare time, she's a boxer and the founder of Queen Bee Boxing.

Nadia's media appearances include The ITV News, *Woman's Hour*, and BBC Radio 4. She has also been featured in all kinds of newspapers and magazines, from *Stylist* and the *Telegraph*, to *Cosmopolitan*, the *Guardian,* and *The Times*.

Nadia has also written a book called *Shy and Mighty: Your Shyness is a Superpower* (DK, 2022) and a book for shy grown ups called *Shy and Mighty* (Quercus, 2022).

When she's not writing or boxing, Nadia works with children and adults to help them step out of the shadows and into a bigger life.

Acknowledgments

Nadia would like to say a big thank you to her husband, Robin, for being very helpful and kind, and to her son, Jacob, for keeping his mum calm under pressure. She'd like to thank her brilliant buddy Kate for being hilarious and totally excellent. And she'd like to thank Brian, her boxing coach, for his support and words of wisdom, and Izzy for being a beaming ray of sunshine.

A massive thank you to everyone at Moon + Bird for believing in her and giving Nadia this incredible opportunity to help quiet kids all over the world. And a special shout out to Nadia's agent, Jason, for being an absolute force!

Thank you to Nadia's friend, Mok, for giving her the time and space to write in his beautiful castle. And to Pam for accompanying Nadia on a gorgeous writing retreat at Gladstone's incredible library.

And finally, Nadia would also like to give Bobby an extra big snuggle because he's very lovely indeed.

MOON ✦ BIRD

We publish empowering and enchanting books to open children's eyes to the wonder of the world and help them grow and thrive. Our beautiful, groundbreaking books encourage curiosity, resilience, and inclusivity, and help kids manage their own feelings and find their own special path in life.

FIND MORE OF OUR BOOKS AT
www.moonandbirdbooks.com